TRUE STEEL

The Story of George Matthew Verity

and His Associates

Blank & Stoller, N. Y.

George M. Verity, Chairman of the Board of Directors, the American Rolling Mill Company.

True Steel

The Story of

GEORGE MATTHEW VERITY

and His Associates

by

CHRISTY BORTH

Author of *Pioneers of Plenty*

ILLUSTRATED

PRINTED IN UNITED STATES OF AMERICA

Again

TO

EVANGELINE

CONTENTS

ILLUSTRATIONS

ILLUSTRATIONS

MILLER'S ANTIQUE MARKET

201 South Broadway
LEBANON, OHIO 45036
(513) 932-8710

SOLD BY | DATE 6-9-11

NAME

ADDRESS

CASH ✓	C.O.D.	CHARGE	ON ACCT.	

1	Iron Steel	2.	00
			13
		2.	13

RECEIVED BY

ALL SALES ARE FINAL - NO REFUNDS

All claims and returned goods MUST be accompanied by this bill.

A 54964

THANK YOU

MILLER'S ANTIQUE MARKET
201 South Broadway
LEBANON, OHIO 45036
(513) 932-6710

ALL SALES ARE FINAL - NO REFUNDS

A 54964

Foreword

IN THE afternoon of his life, the phrase "dean of American steelmakers" fastened itself upon George Matthew Verity, the subject of this biography.

Factually, the phrase is apt; for, as steelmaker, he launched many technological innovations which have affected the lives of all humankind and which are even now affecting the destinies of nations unpredictably.

But the phrase is also inept; for, to use it loosely as description of a man who became a steelmaker accidentally and was a steelmaker only incidentally, is to praise with a faint damn an extraordinarily humane man whose principal role seems to have been that of peacemaker.

As anyone familiar with industrial history knows, the making of steel has been from the start a notoriously stormy business—an industry marked with the scars of titanic struggles for power, branded with the stigma of warmongering, and smudged with the grime of labor strife.

In view of this record, George Verity's success in making steel without strife seems to be sufficient reason for this account of his career.

Addendum

George M. Verity, whose life story is told in these pages, died at the age of 77, on November 6, 1942.

The company he founded began as a sheet rolling mill. With the passing years it grew to become a fully integrated steel producer. As a result, the company changed its name on April 17, 1948 from The American Rolling Mill Company to Armco Steel Corporation in order to describe more accurately its business activities.

I

American April

On the calendar it was April 15, 1865. To the reverent it was Holy Saturday, the day of quiet between Good Friday and Easter. In Ohio it was spring again. Warm rains had lured the last frost out of the rich red earth in the hills of Logan County. In the fields, recently wrested from the wilderness by the bull-tongued plow of the pioneer, the rivulets ran chuckling toward the Mad River. That stream, a lazy mild-mannered stream in midsummer, was now justifying its name—clawing at its banks in its haste to join the churning flood of the Great Miami River in a race to the broad Ohio. On the Mad's upper reaches, not far from the highest point in the state, a horse, drawing a small vehicle, plodded patiently in the mud of a rutted road.

The Reverend Jonathan Verity was riding circuit, composing his Easter sermon as his horse selected its own best path to the next town.

Jonathan Verity was vaguely dissatisfied with the sermon notes he had written in that clear typelike script he used. Somehow words were inadequate for what he felt this morning. For one thing, there was a strange stillness on the land.

"The world is quiet," he thought, "as if spent after weeping."

Just ahead were the rain-lacquered roofs of Zanesfield, his destination. A village rich in Indian lore, its history was a familiar story to him. Here, in 1776, Isaac Zane, who had been stolen in childhood and adopted by Wyandots, married Myeerah, the only daughter of Chief Tarhe, and established in this Huron village the first permanent home of a white man in this part of America. And here, in 1819, the Methodists held their first quarterly conference in the Northwest Territory. Their village church, established in the home of Ebenezer Zane, was part of the Reverend Jonathan's circuit.

The bare bones of the trees above Zanesfield's roofs seemed to be bathed in a colored light. It was as though a fog had been blown away, and Jonathan could see far. But he could not put the vision into words.

Shaking his leonine head with its thick auburn thatch, he tucked his unfinished sermon into an inner pocket and surrendered his mind to the day's delights. He breathed deeply. His eyes feasted on the beauty of dogwood and the cloud-blossom of wild plum and the purple bloom of Judas trees in the woods. A low-driving land wind, flowing rather than blowing, brought the heart-lifting aroma of earth newly turned.

"Things will be better now that winter and warfare are done," he said. "As if in answer to our prayers the Prince of Peace has brought peace again to America. Odd, isn't it, that the war should have ended on Good Friday, four years and a day after it began?"

"It is, indeed."

The reply startled Jonathan. Buoyantly adrift in this tranquil day, he had forgotten he was not alone. Beside him on the thinly cushioned seat of the springless wagon sat Mary Ann who had been his wife for three and a half years now. And between the stern and rugged giant of a man and Mary Ann was Elizabeth, their first-born, a child of two.

The bonds between these three were strong, but this morning the blue eyes beneath the rufous tangle of Jonathan's eyebrows had been looking through and around and beyond these, the frail companions of his arduous migrations in the wilderness "on the Lord's missions." The eyes were restless until they noted the source of that clean odor of turned earth—a partly spaded garden. In it stood a man, resting with arms crossed atop a long-handled spade whose blade was a mirror. As Jonathan Verity drew level, the face above the crossed arms observed politely that it was a good morning.

The morning, said Jonathan, was much better than merely good. It was, he thought, a morning like that first morning when the command for light was gloriously obeyed, or that other first morning when a world, also exhausted after tears, was renewed by the light from a tomb from which a stone had been rolled away.

"It is the morning of a genesis," he said. As he said it, the fugitive words of his Easter sermon came to him and arranged themselves into orderly sentences. In his mind the words and phrases now marched to the cadence of hoofbeats as his horse reached the firmer footing of the village street.

Out of his pocket came his notes and on them he wrote:

"This Easter morn is the dawn once again, the longed-for

April after the four-year winter of war, the resurrection of a nation after a long and terrible night of travail and tears."

In the village the bison-muscled young preacher bounded to earth, lifted his wife and child from the wagon and placed them in the welcoming arms of waiting parishioners. Then he led his horse to the barn and attended to the animal's comfort in the efficient manner he had mastered in the years when he was a farmer before "the call from God" came.

As his hands ministered to the animal's needs, his mind darted back to that July morning five years ago when he had gone to the home of neighbor Jim Beck to cradle oats and had arrived before the Becks had had breakfast. The picture was crystal-clear.

Jim Beck, handing him the *Western Christian Advocate,* had asked him to "sit down and read until breakfast is ready." The first thing he read was an account of the death of a preacher whom he had heard often. He dropped the paper and sat musing. An inner voice asked him why he continued to dodge his duty. There was a struggle in his soul, a struggle against a conviction he had had since his 'teens when he first felt he ought to preach. Then, suddenly, the struggle ended and he said:

"Lord, I will go, and if Thou hast given me but one talent I will use it in Thy service as best I can."

Jim Beck called him to breakfast and "peace, flowing like a river," enfolded him.

"Peace, flowing like a river," he said aloud. It was a favorite phrase of his. He repeated it this morning as he gave his horse a final parting pat. It was his phrase for perfect happiness, the perfect phrase for what he felt today.

On the way to the house he was stopped and told the news—the unbelievably horrible news that blotted out the lambent light of this day.

Mary Ann saw him coming in, staggering, his huge shoulders bowed, his face tight-lipped and drained white. Frightened, she watched his trembling hands fumble inside his coat and withdraw the precious pages of his sermon. Slowly, deliberately, he tore the paper into ribbons and let them spiral to the floor.

"It is the end," he said in a voice grown small and tight. "President Lincoln is dead."

It *was* the end. The "plain people" of Lincoln were certain that his assassination meant the end of their dreamed-of America. Especially these people among whom Jonathan Verity dwelt. Hugging their dreams they had come over the mountains and along the rivers into these Ohio valleys at the beginning of the nineteenth century. First were the Pennsylvanians, both "Dutch" and "Quakers." Then a wave of Virginians, among them the Deatons, Mary Ann's people, a family that had given at least 226 soldiers to the armies of George Washington.

Though famed in these valleys for the gusty laughter of their big-bodied menfolk, there was no joy in this April day for these transplanted Virginia Deatons. Their sorrow was as deep as that of their most numerous neighbors, the Yorkshiremen, among whom were the Veritys.

Of the Veritys, men said they were humorless. They kept pretty much to themselves, worked hard and were not much given to laughter.

"There are no mediocre Veritys," was the verdict of their neighbors. "A Verity is either one thing or another, but never a little of each."

Some manifested individualism bordering on eccentricity. Some showed the touch of genius. Though a bit too religious to be very popular, they were respected for their scrupulous honesty.

That reputation for honesty seemed to have come down with them through the years. The family name had been Verité (truth) when Jonathan's ancestors, followers of John Calvin, fled from persecution in France and settled near Pateley Bridge in the Dale of the Nidd in the West Riding of Yorkshire, England. There these Huguenot emigrés acquired a reputation as dissenters, espousing the left-wing doctrines of John Wesley, who often preached in Pateley Bridge.

In that far time and place, "Methodist" was a word hurled with intent to insult. The Veritys must have been insulted often and may thus have acquired their reputation for "eccentricity" and "near-fanaticism" of which their American neighbors were to remark later.

But what drove them to America was less the contempt of neighbors than the combination of forces which were launched in the world in 1776, when the American Revolution was born amid the scratching of fifty-six pens in Philadelphia, and the Industrial Revolution was born under the banging hammers in the Soho shop of Matthew Boulton, father of mass production, and James Watt, creator of horseless horsepower. The factory manufacture and mechanical horsepower which brought ruin to the small handicraft farm-factories of Yorkshire, jolted Matthew Verity and sent him to America with his wife and five sons in 1831. Having transplanted his family to the fat soil of the Mad River valley not far from the spot where Isaac Zane had settled in 1776, Matthew there fathered two more sons, one of whom was Jonathan.

In the year of Matthew's migration, Ohio was being "opened up." From the south, where New York's Governor DeWitt Clinton had given the signal to begin digging at Middletown, the Miami Canal was creeping northward. From the north came the magic word that the state's first iron highway would stretch from the port of Sandusky through this valley to Springfield and bring the first locomotive west of the Allegheny Mountains.

Jonathan had watched these things as he grew up, had seen them bring to lonely lives of his mud-mired neighbors the bright promise of diminished isolation. Too, he had been troubled as a boy by what he saw and heard as the thousands of brawny bully-boys dug canals daytimes and made the nights riotous with wassail and wenching. There was work a-plenty for "men of God" in this ripsnorting, hell-raising "vineyard of the Lord."

He was in his early twenties on that July morning when, seated on Jim Beck's porch, he had yielded finally to his inner conviction. He was a six-foot giant of a man then, and, though born in America, was "as English in appearance as John Bull." With his great shock of auburn hair, shaggy red eyebrows, and large head set on powerful shoulders, he was formidable-looking save that his frank blue eyes radiated great kindliness. A good farmer, his future seemed to promise prosperity, and there had been much sincere muttering of "Too bad!" among the neighbors when he had tossed that future aside to take up the arduous and thankless travail of the circuit-riding exhorter.

Shortly after he had made his decision, the bellow of Sumter's guns roared the overture of the most tragic of America's wars. He had offered himself for military service, but Lincoln's proclamation exempting ministers of the gospel had brought him back. Received into the Cincinnati Conference of the Methodist Church at Oxford, Ohio, in 1861, he had been appointed to Addison Circuit, which included his family's home. And, in the fall of that first war year, he had married George Deaton's daughter, Mary Ann.

Beautiful and gracious Mary Ann had shared uncomplainingly the ardors of his backwoods ministry. Constantly on the move they were, first on the Addison Circuit, a year on the Lewisburg Circuit, then on the North Lewisburg Circuit. In these years of their constant migrations, their most dependable "home" was the friendly farmhouse of genial George Deaton. There Mary Ann had borne Jonathan's daughter. But on that Holy Saturday when America was riven from end to end by the shock of Lincoln's assassination, this doughty little pioneer mother felt fear. She was expecting her second child, and there were too many muddy miles between her and the warmth of the Deaton home. She knew it when Jonathan stood before her and said, "It is the end."

The skies darkened and the rain came. It drummed on the

roofs and turned the roads into lakes of mire. Listening to the doleful drumming, the plain-talking people of mid-America talked poesy, saying the elements were weeping for Abe. They tramped through the mud in increasing thousands from their homes in the valleys and on the hills. They massed themselves in grief-silenced banks beside the iron rails bearing the train which was bringing home to the prairie bosom the prairie child who had become a martyred President.

On the twenty-second of April, while thousands of Americans slogged through the mud to let their tears mingle with the rain as the Lincoln funeral train wound through Pennsylvania, Mary Ann reached the time of her private travail far from home. Marooned in a sea of mud which is called "Mudsock" to this day, she bore her second child in the home of strangers in the hamlet of East Liberty, near Zanesfield.

The child was a son and she called him George Matthew, after his grandfathers. Jonathan prayed that the boy would follow him into the ministry.

Not the end, as Jonathan feared, but a beginning was this April when George Matthew Verity was born. Until that moment, there had been no American people, no United States. For, until a common grief welded them, Americans had been peoples of many motherlands, and the States had been disunited. True, the rigors of frontier life caused folk like the Virginia Deatons and the Yorkshire Veritys to meet and merge, but the bonds were new and weak, and in many cases four years of internecine war had snapped them. Now, under the hammering of great disaster, America was being forged into unity, spiritually.

Physically, these United States were disunited still. The physical bonds of the sprawling land were mainly the frail fronds of wagon-wheel tracks linking East and West loosely. "The iron road" was the pioneers' phrase for those wheel tracks—an iron road not because it was strong but because its making demanded folk with iron courage in their souls and the salt of irony on their tongues.

There is significance almost mystic in the scattered events of this American April. The Age of Steel was being born then, though Americans still spoke in terms of iron and hoped that iron rails would knit the States into a nation.

As Lincoln's body was being borne across the country almost to the western ends of the iron railways, men remembered that Lincoln himself had standardized the gauges of these rails just a few months before and had thus ended a chaos of rail widths that had threatened to keep America disunited. Others remembered that this same martyred man's vision had been fired by Theodore D. Judah's dream of a transcontinental railroad, and that the resultant iron rails were even then beginning to thrust toward each other from Omaha westward and from the Pacific eastward.

True, the rails were soft iron and makeshift, or at best *imported* steel at $150 in gold per ton. But, in this April:

Up near the top of the United States where white water brawls north into Canada, George Stuntz, hunting gold, picked up an amazingly heavy rock which, gleaming as if diamond-studded, was almost pure hematite. This was the first find of that ore—"Minnesota, No. 1, Bessemer"—which was to be prized by steelmakers.

A bit south of this spot in this same month, Lewis Howell Merritt picked up his first fistful of the red dust which was to make the great Mesabi Iron Range world-famous as the source of American steel.

Farther south, in Chicago, Captain Eben B. Ward was rolling America's first steel rails from America's first steel ingots, produced in Wyandotte, Michigan, by William Durfee, using William Kelley's "pneumatic process."

In New York, Alexander Holley, just returned from England with exclusive rights to use the steelmaking process of Henry Bessemer, was finding himself unable to proceed without infringing on the Kelley patents.

In Birmingham, England, the first commercial open-hearth regenerative furnace was being built by Sir William Siemens to make steel in larger batches with closer control than the Bessemer process could make it.

Near Titusville, Pennsylvania, there was a mad boom of wild-catting in oil that spring—an event linked to the coming Age of Steel through a sharp-eyed Scot and a couple of captains home from the war. The Scot made a quick profit in that oil boom. Looking around for other profits, he learned that Captain James Buchanan Eads had convinced authorities that the Mississippi should be spanned at St. Louis with his newfangled iron bridge. Deciding to become a bridgebuilder, Scot Andrew Carnegie left the pay roll of the Pennsylvania Railroad, organized the Keystone Bridge Company and tempted into his new company that subsequently fabulous steelmaker, Captain William Richard Jones.

It was a time when many momentous things were beginning in America, but the most exciting thing at the moment was the idea of uniting the United States with iron rails and bridges. There were then more than 35,000 miles of rails in the nation, and eight years later the mileage would be doubled to become a tenth of the world's total.

No, that April morning when preachers all over America tore up their Easter sermons was not the end. It was, as Jonathan Verity had called it earlier, "the morning of a genesis."

This American April was—we can see it now!—America's April.

2

Ohio Odyssey

THE Reverend Jonathan Verity loved to preach. Best of all he loved to preach in Newson Chapel, a tiny church set in a grove of maples beside a country lane near the village of Thackery, about ten miles northwest of Springfield. With good reason did he love this spot, for it was here he met and married Mary Ann, whom the Deatons called "the lovely one."

And it was here they brought Mary Ann when she died at the age of 28 on April 29, 1867.

It was, said Jonathan, "a heart-crushing sorrow to have one of the brightest and loveliest of Christian women taken from my side."

He brooded over his loss and deemed it a punishment. In his book, *Fifty-Six Years in the Ministry,* he recorded that this year "was also made memorable by one of the greatest and most precious experiences" in his life.

"For nearly a score of years," he said, "I had lived in the consciousness of a filial relationship to God. During all that time I was happy . . . in the service of God. But when something crossed my path or I was suddenly assailed by some bitter provocation, I was painfully conscious of the springing up within of bitterness, of unholy tempers, of sinful tendencies, and of a disposition when struck by a foe to strike back."

Later that year, as he was "kneeling in the straw about eleven o'clock at night, in deep self-abasement before God," he found peace. As he expressed it:

"God looked upon the travail of my soul and, in infinite mercy, heard and answered my agonizing cry to be made 'a vessel meet for the Master's use.' "

This emotional experience occurred at a camp meeting at Urbana, Ohio. After it happened, Jonathan, a changed man, returned to Addison Circuit and Newson Chapel to be near his children.

After Mary Ann was laid to rest on the southwest slope of the mound that is Newson Chapel Cemetery, her two motherless children were taken down the road, a mile west of the little church, to the home of Grandfather George and Grandmother Hannah Deaton.

Of his mother's death, George remembered little. The sole scar of the hurt was a vague feeling of dread associated with a dim picture of many people coming and going at the tiny Vienna Crossroads parsonage where she died. The hurt was largely forgotten in the happiness with his grandparents.

The Deaton homestead had a large barn with an overhanging loft, and a steep hillside barnyard tilted down toward the road. It was a small boy's concept of heaven, a place offering endless opportunities for exploration and breath-taking discoveries. It was lorded over by a big, jovial man with a vast love of life and a deep understanding of a small boy's problems. For little George's endless questions Grandfather Deaton was never too busy to seek answers.

Beyond and behind the barn and a little to one side of it lay a long sweep of landscaped yard topped by a low-lying house. That house was Grandmother Hannah's province, a place of appetizing odors, good food and down-filled beds.

There was a time when little George tossed fitfully in one of those deep beds as Grandmother Hannah strove day and night to bring him through a siege of typhoid. All through it Grandfather George hovered near, trying to keep him amused, while the Reverend Jonathan prayed.

When the fever left at last and the four-year-old could be taken out of the house, Grandfather George carried him to the barnyard. Introducing the slightly fearful child to a gentle, broad-beamed horse, the man spoke softly to child and animal. Then, having balanced the lad on the animal's back, the protecting hands were withdrawn cautiously—and little George, quivering with delight, wanting to squeal and not daring to, surveyed a startling immense world from the back of a moving horse while his grandfather hovered near, ready to catch him.

This, his first ride, was the beginning of a life-long love of horses.

The Deaton homestead was a favorite gathering place for the neighbors, for Grandfather George, though deeply religious, loved laughter enough to inject humor even into the prayers with which the neighborhood gatherings opened and closed. Once, asking God to "guide us and protect our menfolks from the wiles of Satan," he slyly added after a pause, "and our womenfolks, too," and enjoyed a hearty laugh later when he learned that the kneeling neighbors had almost split their sides trying to control their chuckles.

But happiness at Grandfather's farm was soon over. After two fleeting years of it, the children faced a nervous father who hurriedly introduced their "new mother." Louise King, a former schoolteacher, was prim, pious and "more than exacting." She did not spare the rod, and the trees around the Verity parsonages were always bare of branches that could be utilized for discipline when the Reverend Jonathan received "a new call" and moved on—which was often.

In Jamestown, Ohio, ten miles east of Xenia, where the new family dwelt three full years in two different periods, George first went to school during the second three-year period. There he got his britches birched unforgettably by his "new mother." School was dismissed early one day and, instead of going home, he and another little explorer investigated the alluring mysteries of a distant pond and got much mud on their clothes. The mud was dry when George reached home, so a convenient tree contributed a branch to Stepmother Verity's experiment in dusting him off.

Jonathan took no notice of such trivial things. Deeply immersed in his work, he left the rearing of his children to his wife, and the ex-schoolmistress carried on the rearing according to her own definition of the word. She was profoundly and sincerely afraid the boy might give point to the common contention that "sons of preachers are devil's grandsons."

After that night of kneeling in the straw at Urbana Camp

Meeting, the good Jonathan's temper and combativeness seemed to have entirely disappeared.

Jonathan's superiors in the church Conferences completely dominated him. To son George's way of thinking they used him shabbily. He accepted any post they wished to offer him. Imposed upon, he gloried in submitting to any assignment given him, as he considered it God's will.

As George grew older he had an increasing realization of what was going on. The Reverend Jonathan would come home from Conference full of praise for its presiding officers, and would justify their action in giving him an even poorer assignment than the previous one. The boy, catching the distressed look in his harried stepmother's tired eyes, would feel his throat tighten with the bitterness of anger, as he had attended these Conferences on several occasions and had seen his father meekly submit to injustice.

As a result of Jonathan's willingness to accept any call to duty as he saw it, the family was on the move almost constantly. "Home" to George was a sixty-mile-wide strip of Ohio, extending over a hundred miles of hills and valleys between Springfield and Cincinnati. Packing boxes were a regular part of the household equipment. They were always either in use or in readiness. From the time he was seven until he was fifteen, the boy did not spend more than three consecutive years in any one community. In the first twenty years of his life he lived in Cincinnati four times.

During one of the family's early periods in Cincinnati, the famous Women's Temperance Crusade got under way. Launched in Hillsboro, three days before Christmas 1873, it was advanced by exhorters of many denominations with a series of revivals. Properly primed, the good women surged into the streets to kneel in semicircles on the sidewalks before the swinging doors of saloons. There they prayed, publicly, loud and long. Stepmother Verity was one of the leaders of these bands, which developed into the W. C. T. U. She was increasingly active in assisting her spouse shout the drowsy souls of sinners awake in those endless revivals of his.

Because his father was so completely absorbed in this church work, and because George was never in any one school long enough to develop permanent companionships, he was a lonely lad.

Thus, this friendless little fellow had his first lessons in self-sufficiency. He tinkered with a kit of tools. His proudest possession was a scroll saw, earned by selling magazine subscriptions. He also had a wooden bow-gun. For ammunition he used nails, and his father knew so little about the boy's doings that he boasted: "George is always building—building so much we can't keep a nail in the house."

The observation was not entirely wrong. George *did* build. In Jamestown, when he was fourteen, he built a kite, and a lantern, light enough to be supported by it, yet designed to stand the necessary wind pressure. He sent his invention aloft one starless night and was very happy when he saw a Xenia newspaper's report of the excitement caused by a strange light dancing in the eastern sky.

Jonathan's annual salary never exceeded $800 in the early

years of that Ohio odyssey and was often much less than that. There were five mouths to be fed out of that pittance, for another child had been born to the Veritys. The family was always hard pressed. So George had to help early. He earned his first dollar in Fairmount when he was ten. He had fallen into an open stairway while playing in a partially built schoolhouse, and had sprained his right wrist. A sympathetic neighbor offered to pay him for whitewashing her fence. He did the work with his left hand, and accepted a dollar in payment in high glee.

His favorite game was baseball, but he found little time to play it or anything else after the family returned to Jamestown in his twelfth year. For his father bought a cottage with a few acres, a horse, a cow and some pigs, and the boy's days and nights were full of work and study thereafter. In winter work began before dawn with the milking. George, not liking the dark, got the milking done so quickly that his elders were pleased but puzzled.

Until he was fourteen, each year was brightened by a summer of happiness on Grandfather Deaton's farm, where his companion was his young uncle, Willis.

To George and Hannah Deaton, this slender, spunky redhead of Mary Ann's was "their" boy. Their influence upon his character was deep. One thing they gave him was a strong love of the land.

In George's fourteenth summer, his father took him into the harvest field on a parishioner's farm and showed him how to bind sheaves of grain by hand. Harvesting machines, introduced by Cyrus McCormick on a Virginia farm in the year of Grandfather's migration to America, were then revolutionizing agriculture, and the world's largest producer of such machinery was a factory in near-by Springfield. But the machines still required hands for the binding.

The binder's job, called "making a hand," demanded a skill of which Jonathan was a proud possessor. Working in the fields together, father and son, as instructor and pupil, learned to understand each other better. Both were very proud when the boy, having quickly mastered this man's job, was paid a man's wage—two dollars a day.

Now the fourteen-year-old was certain he had become a man. His assurance was the look of pride in his father's eyes.

At this time, too, he reached an unexpected understanding with his stepmother. He and his half sister, then aged four, had quarreled over some trivial incident. The girl's mother picked up a riding whip conveniently near to defend her child and rushed at the boy. He started to flee. Suddenly, something deep inside him made him stop at the door and turn about and say, with a cool defiance and self-assurance he could never explain:

"Don't you touch me!"

It was a command, with a ring of icy spicules that flabbergasted that good but sorely overworked woman. She stood as if rooted to the spot, her mouth open and her upraised arm slowly falling to her side. So they stood for a moment, surveying each other. Then the boy turned slowly and walked out of the house. Dazed by what he had done, he walked in a straight line, on and on, saying to himself:

"I'll never be afraid of anyone or anything again."

He was climbing over a fence and exulting over this newly discovered hidden power within himself when he heard his father call:

"George, come back! I want to talk to you."

"I'll come back, Father," he replied, "but she must never touch me again."

And she didn't. There was peace between the boy and his stepmother thereafter. They learned to respect and understand each other. In time their understanding came close to mother-and-son affection.

In after years he often said that the incident marked a distinct turning point in his life. "It would be impossible to set a value on its influence," he said. One of the chief values derived from this, his "declaration of independence," was the conviction, born of the incident, that there was within him a mysterious reserve of strength which he could call upon to help him meet any situation.

When he was sixteen, the family moved again, this time to Georgetown, a pleasant county-seat village whose residents were then trying to be proud again of the fact that this had been the boyhood home of Ulysses S. Grant. For this was 1881, and "Black Friday" and its ugly aftermath of scandal that touched President Grant had gone a decade down in discarded calendars.

Georgetown was—and is—a gracious little town, and George Verity tasted real happiness in it. Enrolled in high school, the lithe, auburn-haired, blue-eyed lad discovered his first real opportunity to enjoy the constant companionship of others.

He had made a bobsled. Since it was the only one in town, he was a popular boy when there was snow on White Oak Hill, west of the village. Coasting was mostly done after the early hour of winter sunset, and darkness added to the thrill of the downhill flight the sharp spice of danger. As the sled was built for two, it usually bore a girl, fluttery with excitement and some fear, and a boy, brave and protective. So George for the first time met the girls and boys together and found the experience pleasant.

Pleasant, too, was his companionship with Rufus Colfax Phillips whom he met here. Rufus was a merry lad whom the Georgetown youths called "Duce." The plotter of many pranks, the leader and idol of his age group, Duce Phillips was born in Georgetown on May 1, 1865. Returning to the community after a considerable absence, he met George.

"Hello, Red," he said, and from that moment the effervescent Duce and the quiet but impulsive and energetic Red were companions. They worked together one summer in the harvest fields—worked hard and enjoyed the experience. They learned at first hand about that great hunger the human heart has for an opportunity to show loyalty and how strongly the heart responds when the opportunity is offered. It was a lesson that was to serve them well.

They were delighted to discover they had been born only nine days apart.

Together, they attended school and Sunday school, church

services and prayer meetings. They squired girls together at strawberry socials. They rode horseback side by side and dreamed of the great and dazzling future they would share after graduation from Georgetown High School.

At last, the longed-for day of release arrived. Six boys, their unruly hair slicked down, stood on the stage of the high-school auditorium, trying to appear brave and grown-up in their too-tight, too-stiff collars and their too-new blue serge suits. Beside them were seven girls, star-eyed with excitement, the peach-pink of their flushed cheeks accented by the fluffy whiteness of frilly dresses that had been labored over for weeks. The "brave" boys quaking and the "frail" girls cool as cream jugs in a spring-house, the thirteen graduating youths blinked into the white light of "incandescent" gas burners beating down on them as the Reverend Jonathan Verity took his time about asking God's blessing in that booming baritone of his.

The Reverend Jonathan was in fine fettle this night. He had done well in Georgetown; so well, in fact, that the townsfolk were a little resentful of the Conference rule limiting a preacher's stay to three years in one place. But the Conference heads were also beginning to show signs of appreciation. They had now called him to McKendree Chapel in Cincinnati's East End.

On this important night Jonathan's big heart was stretched to bursting with gratitude—and he took a lot of time to make certain his thanks were heard and understood where he was directing them.

At last it was George's turn to deliver the salutatory address, a dissertation on "Pernicious Literature," which he had written out, labored over and memorized in every waking moment for weeks. He knew it now as well as he knew the feel of his tongue against his teeth.

Or did he?

His tongue and teeth suddenly felt unaccountably foreign as he groped for the next word. A whispered line from Pattie King, a lass sitting next to him, saved him—and he was off with a triumphant flourish to the climax. There was a split second, centuries long, of dead silence. Then a crash of applause. As he sat down under the class motto, "Onward and Upward Aim," he felt within himself the renewed assurance that he could meet whatever might come to him with equanimity.

Ada Lyon, the valedictorian, wound up the ceremony, and the crowd was on its feet, milling about, chattering, laughing. And a golden moment for these thirteen youngsters slipped down the corridor of time, lost in a flood of talk and laughter.

The gas lights were turned down. Their white light became yellow, then blue. The blue flames trembled before the onrush of the darkness which, poised and waiting, now rushed in.

Outside, it was spring again, and the cloud of plum and dogwood and Judas tree blossoms drifted north over the land. Red and Duce, pledging eternal companionship, parted. In the Verity parsonage, the packing cases were ready for the move to Cincinnati.

It was April, 1883.

3

Preparation without Plan

AT Cincinnati, after the packing cases were empty and stored, the Reverend Jonathan opined it would be nice indeed if his son should see fit to go to Ohio Wesleyan University at Delaware, Ohio, and prepare to follow in the paternal footsteps. George, thinking of those packing cases stored against the next move, concluded that the paternal footsteps were too migratory.

Toward the end of the summer he told his father of this decision. Though Jonathan was obviously deeply disappointed by the revelation, the large-souled man generously agreed to let the boy chart his own life.

"What do you plan to do, George?" he asked.

"I don't know, Father," he replied. "You see, I don't know what I *can* do."

It was hard for the boy to plan a career. In fourteen schools scattered throughout southwestern Ohio he had picked up a rag, tag and bobtailed education. He was certain there were serious gaps in this hodgepodge of educational odds and ends. True, he was eighteen and had graduated from high school, but he wasn't sure he was prepared to seek a job.

So, at the suggestion of his father, he presented his problem to the faculty of Cincinnati's famous Woodward High

School. "Old Woodward" it was affectionately called because it had nurtured so many illustrious sons and daughters of the "Queen City of the West."

His case was indeed a problem for Old Woodward's faculty; for, though a high-school graduate, he knew almost nothing at all about some subjects considered essential for high-school credits. Preparing a course of studies planned to telescope three-year courses into two years, they admitted him in the fall.

Cincinnati was then at the peak of its queenly glory as seventh in size of the nation's cities. As a natural gateway for river-borne commerce between North and South, it had grown from a village of less than a thousand inhabitants in 1800 to a busy city of almost a quarter-million in the eighties. Though its growth had slackened now, it was thriving in many ways not noted in census statistics—in music and art, in the building and endowing of schools and hospitals. In its degree of civic consciousness, it was unique among American cities; for this was the time when, private enterprise shunning the project, the community built a railroad—the only first-class railroad owned by a city in the United States.

The city was giving leaders to the nation, such leaders as the Taft and Longworth families produced. It was the site of daring pioneering in industrial relations: the company founded by William Procter and James Gamble was then setting standards of employer-employee relations which are copied still. The Queen City was an ideal spot for George's education.

McKendree Chapel and parsonage were in about the center of the town's East End, and young George walked to and from

Woodward High School, a daily jaunt of some eight to ten miles.

He was not happy at home, and he was less happy at Old Woodward. The faculty's solution of his problem meant starting him as a freshman which was hardly conducive to the happiness of a youth who had done man's work for man's wages since he was fourteen and was now being associated with much younger boys.

He put up with it silently and stoically until the Christmas holidays, when he proposed to tell his father he wanted to quit school and go to work.

During the holidays, however, he overheard a conversation which slanted him in a new direction. Mentioned in the talk were the words "business college." He had never heard of a business college, but after an investigation he decided that such a course was just what he wanted and needed.

Approached with this new and unexpected request, the Reverend Jonathan referred again to his dream of his son in a pulpit, but added he supposed George should have the privilege of deciding for himself.

Thus the Richard Nelsons, father and son, got him into their Nelson's Business College in January, 1884. The school, which stood on the site later occupied by the Sinton Hotel, specialized in a general business course requiring eight months of study. Young George's thirsty mind fairly gulped the Nelson offerings, and he began to think of the future with himself sitting serenely in the middle of it, bewhiskered, besought and, by turns, benign and ice-eyed—a banker.

The Reverend Jonathan thought he could help at that point. George Larkin, the president of the Lafayette Bank, was an outstanding Methodist. Jonathan took George to see him. Preacher and banker had so many things to discuss they almost forgot young George. Oh yes! A job. Application blank. Fill it and sign it. And that was that.

The Cincinnati Conference of the Methodist Church owned and operated, in a sylvan spot on the banks of the Little Miami near Loveland, a summer colony called Epworth Heights. It comprised summer cottages, an auditorium, a summer hotel and a general store. Each year a different church or group in the Conference was granted the concession to operate hotel and store.

In the summer of 1884, the concession fell to McKendree Chapel, and George, on vacation from Nelson's, was put to work as room clerk and assistant in the store.

Helping in the store one day, he looked up from a list of groceries into the most attractive eyes he had ever seen. They fascinated him. He stared. And their owner smiled. So he assembled the young lady's grocery order and, though it was not large, insisted he *must* carry it for her. She graciously accepted his offer. Her family's cottage, she said, was just across the ravine. George suggested the long route around the ravine. That gave him time to learn she was Miss Jennie Standish, one of the fifteen-year-old twin daughters of W. C. Standish, a Cincinnati grocer. Her father was seriously ill at the time, so George did not meet him.

Returning to the store George was busy with mental arithmetic having nothing to do with grocery bills or Nelson's bookkeeping lessons. It had something to do with what fifteen will be when nineteen is twenty-one. It was a jumble of figures all mixed up in a fluff of light brown hair "floating like a vapor on the soft summer air," and a girl whose family called her "Jean."

Toward midsummer, George and Jean had an "understanding." She would spend the next three years growing up. He would get a job, work hard, save his money, and then they would marry. The moonlight can be as lovely on the Little Miami as on the Wabash, especially when seen through four young eyes in two young heads held close together and shaping one plan.

Plan? Before the summer's end, Jean's father died. Where was the plan now? George offered his assistance to the grief-stricken family, and the widow and her three daughters accepted his offer. He virtually took charge of the household until after the funeral from the Standish home in Newport, Kentucky, and was a trusted friend of the family thereafter.

When Jean's father died at the age of fifty, he left his widow in something of a predicament. Her father, William Holt, had founded and built a wholesale and retail grocery business on the site of the present Federal Building in Cincinnati. It was a family institution which had been taken over by her husband after her father's death and had been moved to Pearl Street near Broadway. Now its directing head was gone and there was only her elder daughter to keep an eye on the business as bookkeeper. She would either have to sell the business, which was unthinkable, or find a good manager, which would be difficult.

One day, just before George had finished his course at Nelson's, Mrs. Standish almost bowled him over by asking him if he would consider managing her store. He had been thinking of that job in a bank, but before he knew what had happened, he was the bookkeeper and manager of a grocery store and oyster depot.

In 1884, the place where the W. C. Standish Grocery Company stood was the pulsating heart of Cincinnati's shopping district. Two blocks down Broadway was dockland where scores of grunting, bellowing river packets were loading and unloading cargoes at all times. On Pearl Street between Broadway and Sycamore was the famous old Pearl Street Market.

Uphill and next to Pearl Street was Third Street's financial center at which George had been aiming. Fourth Street was "the top of the hill," an avenue of hotels and retail stores with residential districts at the ends. Fifth Street was "way up town"; indeed, it was almost out of town.

The Cincinnati courthouse was a mess of charcoal and ashes that year. On March 28 several slayers were convicted of manslaughter when most people expected a verdict of murder. The people disagreed with the court, and in the disagreement, which lasted several days, the courthouse was burned down, five were killed and 138 wounded.

The people showed a strange predilection for disagreeable conduct that year. Crimes of violence were commonplace in Cincinnati, which was beginning its long career of civic corruption under the notorious Boss George Barnsdale Cox. During a bitterly fought strike in Ohio's Hocking Valley, a handful of desperate miners set fire to underground coal deposits at New Straitsville and started a subterranean blaze which was still going strong a half-century later. In New York, during the stormy presidential campaign between Blaine and Cleveland, the people, maddened by rumors of political corruption, surged through the streets, threatening revolution. Americans were in an ugly mood after a sudden panic brought on by the machinations of Ferdinand Ward, "the Pied Piper of Wall Street," who led hundreds of investors to ruin.

It was a time of turbulence. Ideas which had been stirring in 1865 were now becoming forces altering the shape of human life. There was the idea of harnessing the strange force of electricity. At the moment of George Verity's birth, the idea of the practical dynamo had been emerging from the minds of Wilde, von Siemens and Pacinotti; the British photographer, Joseph Wilson Swan, had attempted to convert electricity into light with a carbon filament; and Thomas Alva Edison, who was to succeed where Swan failed, was a shabbily dressed tramp operator applying his inventive ingenuity to devices for electrocuting rats in a Cincinnati telegraph office. Edison's lamps, which by the spring night of George's graduation at Georgetown were astounding New Yorkers, now in 1884 were being shown at Cincinnati's Fall Festival, where George saw the amazing things for the first time.

The lamps were the talk of the town, a novelty to add to those recent marvels, the electric rail car and the telephone.

Just after George's arrival in Cincinnati, many amazed

Americans had stood under the June sun in Chicago, saying again and again, "Will wonders never cease?" and "What is the world coming to?" What they were witnessing was the birth of electric traction. What they actually saw was "the Judge," an electric locomotive, growling around a circular track, pulling carloads of passengers, drawing its power mysteriously from a "third rail." Later that year, many Cincinnatians took passage on river packets to see "the Judge" in operation at an electrical fair in Louisville, Kentucky.

George heard men speculate about the work which electric energy might one day do, but he had little time to indulge in such daydreams, and most certainly no premonition of the part he would one day play in making that form of energy work for mankind.

Around the corner from the Standish store there was a drugstore boasting one of the city's twenty-five hundred telephones. Store-manager Verity used the device several times, but he did not like it. "It squeaked too much and really didn't go anywhere," he said. Besides, one had to shout into the device. And George had little occasion or inclination to shout about anything.

In a letter written to Duce about this time, he expressed a longing to marry Jean, migrate to Florida and grow oranges. A preacher, visiting his father, had fired the young man's mind with verbal pictures of life in Florida. Writing to Phillips, he said, "I'm tired of working like a dog and making nothing. I want to get somewhere, where I can make every lick count."

No, he had little occasion to shout. Not that his pay was poor! Fifteen dollars a week was not bad for a nineteen-year-old beginner in those times. But the hours! Open store at five in the morning, six days a week. Keep books. Watch accounts. Look over "drummers'" wares; do the buying; plan advertising; wait on customers and placate squawkers. Wheedle deadbeats. Try to close doors at nine, five days a week, and midnight on Saturdays. That's a ninety-nine-hour work week—if you don't try to balance books after closing hours, which George did. Small wonder that he later took a lead in shortening the hours of labor for others!

He had not been on this treadmill very long when he decided to save time and expense by living at the store—literally. Rigging up a combination of office and living quarters in a back room, he was able not only to handle his many duties, but save time and a little money, and—what was most important then—find time to see Miss Jean more often. For it was the fascinating Jean who really kept him in harness in the grocery business which, he was discovering, was not to his liking.

It was hard going. George was young, and the older clerks—older in years and service—were naturally resentful about having to take orders from a younger man. He had to handle them with rare tact. They learned, however, that this diplomatic lad was far from soft. Take the case of the skipping oysterman, for example.

Part of the Standish business was the operation of a wholesale oyster depot with a delivery system serving most of the town's retailers of seafood. One day George learned that his oyster deliveryman had contracted to work for a competitor and, though still working for the Standish store, was quietly signing up the store's customers to string along with him when he changed jobs.

The Verity temper flared. Almost as quickly as it flared, it cooled, and the skipping oysterman was quietly but quickly dismissed. Then, in the dead of an unusually heavy winter, George took over the route himself and finished out the season without the loss of a customer.

Disagreeable experiences such as this one made him feel that, in the grocery business, he was just a square peg rattling loosely in a large round hole.

It was a small store at the other end of Pearl Street Market which changed that belief into conviction. He watched that small store open, saw its business grow, correctly appraised its significance. It was operated by an extremely popular young man whose ready wit bubbled so freely off his blarneying tongue that many believed him to be Irish and called him Barney.

This Barney was about as Irish as *Sauerbraten mit Nudeln,* for his father came from Hanover, Germany, in 1817, and his mother's family name was Schlebbe. Barney's father was in the dry-goods business on Central Avenue opposite Betts Street until his death in 1880. Barney went to school until 1873, when he was thirteen. Then he became a clerk in the Northern Pacific Tea Company store, moved on to the store of the Imperial Tea Company and, in 1883, opened up the first of his own little stores with the big title: Great Western Tea Company—Bernard Henry Kroger, proprietor.

By 1887 it was obvious to George that the Kroger stores, then spreading in Cincinnati, had a merchandising formula with the seeds of great success in it. So he had a heart-to-heart talk with Mrs. Standish, whom he was now calling "Mother." He explained why Kroger, buying in large quantity for a chain of stores, could sell cheaper than the Standish store could buy. He advised her to sell her store if a buyer could be found.

Mrs. Standish was at first reluctant. The store had been in her family for two generations and, with George and Jean planning to marry, she had hoped it would remain in the family for another generation. But she came around finally to acceptance of her prospective son-in-law's suggestion and told him to look for a buyer.

"But what will you do?" she asked.

"I don't know," he said.

The broad experience of three years of management had been valuable. Of that he was certain. But he had not the faintest notion of what his next step would be. All he had was the inner conviction that, when the time came to make the step, it would be the right step to take.

Late in the summer of 1887, while he was closing up the accounts preparatory to turning over the store to the purchaser, the postman brought a letter that pointed to the next step.

The letter contained no clew as to the nature of the business. It was merely an invitation to George Verity to call upon the writer at his earliest convenience in a law office in the Johnson Building at Fifth and Walnut Streets. The signature was "H. P. Lloyd."

"Who is H. P. Lloyd?" George wanted to know.

4

Education in the Eighties

THE Major sat in his office in the Johnson Building and looked sourly at an accountant's report of a business of which he was now the sole owner, but to which he had never been able to give much time or attention. He stroked his beard, the memento of his service under General Ambrose E. Burnside, whose name had been associated with this form of facial foliage. Whenever the Major stroked his beard it was a sign that he was in deep thought.

"Stuck!" jeered the imps of doubt darting through the unwonted gloom of the Major's thinking.

"Damn!" said the Major.

His partner, the Judge, looked up inquiringly. The Major chose to ignore the unasked question. No use telling Judge Bill about this. He would only laugh. And, at the moment, Major Harlan Page Lloyd was in no mood to enjoy the booming laughter of Judge William Howard Taft.

A good lawyer who shone in bankruptcy cases as an associate of Judge Bill's father, the Honorable Alphonso Taft, Major Lloyd had acquired sole ownership of a sheet-metal factory—and he admittedly knew little about sheet metal and less about a factory.

It was not that the Major was ignorant. No, he knew much

about many things. After graduation from Hamilton College in 1859, he had taught school while studying law in Bloomfield, New Jersey. Then, when Fort Sumter was fired upon, he had snapped his books shut and gone to war as a lieutenant of cavalry. Leaving the service long enough to be admitted to the bar in Albany, New York, in December, 1861, he had enlisted again, this time as a private in an artillery battery. After service under whiskery General Burnside, he had been commissioned captain of cavalry and ordered to join the Army of the Potomac.

Near Winchester on August 21, 1864, he had been shot and carried off the field to die. Then he had astonished everyone—himself included—by recovering in time to campaign for the re-election of Lincoln. In the following spring he had marched with Sheridan in the Shenandoah, assisted in the defeat of Jubal Early and, commissioned major, had participated in the battles leading to Lee's surrender.

He had learned this military business so well that General George A. Custer had urged him to join his famous Seventh Cavalry (later wiped out at Little Big Horn), but the Major, deciding to get on with law, had moved to Cincinnati after his discharge in August, 1865.

In 1869 he had attained national recognition in a case in which he represented some emancipated slaves seeking to recover an inheritance wrested from them on a technicality, and had not only won the case but had induced the courts to recognize the validity of slave marriages.

Major Lloyd was a scholarly man, much in demand as a public speaker. He had traveled extensively in Europe, had married the daughter of President John H. Raymond of Vassar College, and had turned down many attractive offers to hold public office. Knowing much about many things, he knew enough to realize he would have to seek a manager for his sheet metal factory now that its manager, his former partner in the business, had sold out to him and announced his intention to leave.

But where was he to look for a manager? He stroked his whiskers—and awakened a slumbering thought. Why hadn't he thought of it before? Certainly the accountants who had prepared this report should be able to help him.

Yes, the head of the firm of accountants told him, they might be able to help. Here, for instance, is a list of able young men recommended by Nelson's Business College. Ah! here's a good possibility. George Verity's the name . . . Methodist minister's son . . . did a fine job of managing the Standish store for Standish's widow . . . understand the store is being sold and young Verity is staying on only long enough to help the new owner. Maybe you can interest this young fellow, Major. Here's the name and address. . . . Oh, no bother at all, Major! Thank *you,* Major!

A few days later George Verity met Major Lloyd. After formalities were out of the way, the Major said he had become owner of a factory located on the Public Landing and, since he knew nothing whatever about the business, he was desirous of obtaining the services of a good manager.

"The principal product of the factory is sheet-metal roofing," he said.

George concealed his sudden recognition of the fact that he had lived under roofs since the day of his birth but knew as little about them now as he had known then. But apparently the Major was not concerned about his ignorance of roofs, for he was saying:

"The factory is between Sycamore and Main, next door to the Consolidated Boat Store Company, two doors from the Freiberg & Workum distillery—if you know where that is."

Not being what was then called "a drinking man," George was not interested in distilleries, but he knew about where the boat store was situated.

"Don't drink, eh? Good!" said the Major, hastening to explain that the factory bought iron and steel sheets and converted them into building materials, such as sheathing, roofing and siding. He added that he had interests also in similar factories in Birmingham, Chicago, St. Louis and New Orleans, but that the Cincinnati factory, in which he had had a minor interest, had become his problem when it went into receivership and he bought out his associate and assumed the company's debts.

This associate, he explained, was Louis L. Sagendorph, an inventive genius with the usual inventor's aversion for the dull routine of management.

"Perhaps you are familiar with some of the products of the Sagendorph genius," the Major continued, "especially that form of sheet-metal siding which, painted red, enables a frame house to masquerade as brick.

"Unfortunately for me," said the Major, "Mr. Sagendorph is more interested in the conception of newer ideas than in staying on and attempting to make money with the good ones already developed. He wants to go to Philadelphia to broaden his field of operations. He has agreed to remain four months to introduce a new manager to his duties. Then he is determined to leave."

The Major was stroking his whiskers again. Suddenly he stopped and looked his young visitor squarely in the eyes.

"I've got this business on my hands," he said, "and I'm looking for someone to manage it. Its management will not be easy. It's in receivership. I'm the receiver as well as the owner, and will give a manager all the help I can. I've looked into your record. I believe you are capable. I'd like you to go down to the shop, meet Sagendorph, look the place over, then decide."

George Verity walked down to the Public Landing, thinking . . . thinking that he had never so much as seen the inside of a factory in his twenty-two years . . . thinking of how very little he knew about machinery of any kind . . . thinking of what the difference might be between sheathing and siding, tin plate and terneplate . . . but thinking, too, that he had not been pushed around all these years for nothing—at least he knew how to learn. He knew the way to seem as wise as an owl is to be as mum as a stuffed one.

So he went down to the Public Landing, and kept his mouth shut and his eyes and ears open as Sagendorph talked and the two of them explored the factory.

Once more he stood before the Major. Once more he felt that deep conviction that he need fear nothing.

"I'd like to try this job," he said.

"Good!" said the Major. "I'll help you all I can. Would a salary of—say—twelve hundred a year suit you?"

It would indeed, he replied, trying to hang on to enough of that stuffed-owl aplomb to mask his elation, for this offer was almost twice as much as he had been earning.

After he got out of range of the Major's eye, he fairly flew across the Ohio River to Jean and asked her to set the wedding date as early as possible.

They were married in Grace Methodist Episcopal Church in Newport, Kentucky, on October 19, 1887. To be best man at his friend's wedding, Duce Phillips came down from Columbus where he was then working. The bridesmaid was Jean's twin sister, Fannie.

"George," said Duce when he saw the bridesmaid, "you're a friend indeed!" Exactly one year later, to the day, sister Fannie became Mrs. Rufus Colfax Phillips.

At about the time when George and his bride were setting up housekeeping in a second-floor flat of the then new Masonic Temple Building in Newport, a smiling, twinkling-eyed Irishman was mounting the stairs at 15-16-17 Public Landing to the second-floor office of the L. L. Sagendorph Iron Roofing and Corrugating Company.

Here, he had heard, there was need for a good stationary engineer. Presenting himself to Mr. Sagendorph who was still on the job, he was asked:

"Are you a good one?"

"That I am," he replied, presenting his credentials which

stated that he was John Hogan, born February 15, 1855, "a first-class engineer and a faithful, dependable workman."

John Hogan was hired. The vacancy he filled had come about by accident in a general reduction of personnel instituted in a frantic effort to cut operating costs.

When engineer Hogan reported for work he looked around and wondered why he had been hired. Of about a score of workmen in the place, most of them seemed to him to be only polishing the seats of their pants. There seemed to be no foreman. There was little work in progress. Spying a tinsmith tidying his workbench, Hogan asked:

"What's going on here?"

"Nothing much," said tinsmith John Schueller. "You see, Mr. Sagendorph is a genius. Mind you, he's a good man to work for, but he hates business details. I know! I've worked for him since I was eighteen and I'm twenty-eight now. He's got a lot of good ideas, like the sheet-metal imitations of brick, stone and wood siding we make here, but he sure needs a practical man to make a business out of his inventions."

"Why are you all sitting around?" asked Hogan.

"No orders," Schueller replied. "We often sit around waiting for orders. Sometimes Sagendorph comes in and is surprised to see us sitting. He asks us why and we say, 'No orders.' 'Why,' he says, 'I thought we had plenty of orders.' Then he says, 'Stay where you are, boys; I'll go out and drum up some orders.' And he almost always does. I sure hope the new boss pays more attention to getting business."

"Seen the new boss yet?"

"Yeah. Young fellow. Redhead. Looks like a boy. Nice big mustache but he still looks like a boy. Name's George Verity. Major Lloyd—he's the real boss—hired him because he done well running the Widow Standish's store over on Pearl Street. Understand Sagendorph is to help him for a few months, then he's on his own. Looks like he's got a real job on his hands."

George, having wound up his duties at the store, reported for work a few days later. The men were still shining their pants. Not only were there no orders, no work, and no foreman, but there was no one in charge of buying or selling, no one to handle correspondence, no bookkeeper—not even an office boy. There was an accumulation of neglected duties, all of which he had to begin to handle himself.

"Looks like this young man's got a job on his hands," said the boys in the shop.

It was a task for a titan. Night after night George Verity went home, utterly worn out, wondering if he hadn't overreached his ability in tackling this unfamiliar business.

After George had been in the shop a fortnight, Hogan sauntered into the tinshop to discuss him with Schueller.

"Well, John," said Hogan, "do you think you'll go to Philadelphia with Sagendorph?"

"I don't know," Schueller replied. "This new manager doesn't know much about this business, but he's young and seems willing and anxious to learn. I think I'll decide after I see how he gets along."

And, after a reflective pause, Schueller continued:

"You know, Hogan, there's one thing I can't figure out about this fellow. He's friendly and easy to get along with and not the kind of boss who makes you feel you ought to keep your distance; still, I notice all of us, even the old bucks, are calling him *Mister* Verity instead of George like we did at first. I can't figure it out."

"It's a gift," said Hogan, "and he has it. I liked him the first time I set eyes on him, and I think I'll stick."

Shortly after this conversation Schueller made up his mind. He was working on a building in Covington, making an old roof weather-tight with some muslin and heavy paint, a process which Sagendorph had developed. The building superintendent inspected the work and said he did not think it would keep out the rain. George was summoned. He inspected the work carefully. Then he said:

"If John Schueller did the work, I *know* it's going to be right. He knows more about this kind of work than anyone else."

Reporting the incident to Hogan, Schueller said:

"As long as he wants me I'll go along with him. I figure you can't go wrong going along with a man who knows how to listen to you and makes you feel your opinion is as good as his. He makes you feel you're working *with* him instead of *for* him—gives you a chance to make or break yourself. I'll stick."

"So will I," said Hogan.

Both of them did—for fifty years.

Sagendorph left and on April 21, 1888, George assumed the full responsibilities of manager of the little factory. As Hogan and Schueller had predicted, he had his hands full—buying sheet iron and steel, fabricating it into building materials, selling the finished product, answering all correspondence in longhand, converting office chaos into orderly bookkeeping, handling men who knew he knew less about the business than they did.

As if that were not enough for the tyro, there was, right at the beginning, the serious problem of an abnormally large inventory of sheet metal that had been bought on a falling market, an accumulation of raw material that had almost crushed the business, and which had to be disposed of as quietly as possible.

To the Major's order to get rid of the stuff, George replied, "I'm afraid I'm not much of a salesman."

The fear was not, however, justified. Though the young manager had four veteran competitors within a six-block area, he succeeded in selling so much of the accumulated iron that in the second year the Major was able to pay off all debts and get the company out of receivership.

Major Lloyd rapidly revised his former poor opinion of the business that he had acquired through trying to help his friend Sagendorph. When George suggested that he really needed a bookkeeper, the Major listened sympathetically.

"You shall have a good one," he said, uttering a better prophecy than he realized. For, two days before Christmas of 1889, William Frank Rambo reported for duty and began a term of more than fifty years of continuous service.

The next addition to the staff was white-haired Willie Knight, the office boy who later developed into one of Cincinnati's first traffic officers.

These were days of high adventure for the little group—not more than a score of people all told, who never knew from one week to the next whether there would be enough cash in the till to fill the pay envelopes. On Saturdays, when farmers congregated at near-by Pearl Street Market, routine duties in the factory were dropped and every member of the staff became a salesman. Since some of the customers spoke German only, Schueller had often to lay tin-snips and soldering iron aside and act as interpreter.

Then, from across the river, there came a bright apple-cheeked girl who had taken a business course and wanted a job as stenographer. Women stenographers were at that time comparatively rare, but George talked the Major into hiring her. There were never any regrets about the hiring of Emma Amelia Rheinhart, for she became the best salesman of the lot of them.

But manager Verity soon realized he would have to find someone who could devote full time to selling. With the Major's approval, he wrote to Duce Phillips, now his brother-in-law, asking if he would not like to join him in this business adventure. The letter was not at first particularly interesting to Duce, who was prospering as a star salesman for the Columbus Buggy Company. Buggies were at that time selling fast enough at $200 each to convince young Phillips he was in a business with a great future—a much more attractive future than iron roofs and downspouts and such.

Ultimately, however, friendship was the deciding factor, and Duce joined his boyhood companion as sales manager.

Relieved of some of his duties, Verity was able to devote

more attention to management. At the end of the third year he had saved $500 out of his salary. Would the Major sell him a block of stock in the company? The Major would—gladly!

This was his first investment of any kind. A little later he made his second one. Learning of a German tinker in Covington, Kentucky, who had invented and patented a spiral twisted pipe, called Polygon, which was stronger and more attractive than the plain or corrugated downspouts then in use, he made a deal with the inventor for the purchase of his patents.

To provide the necessary machinery and equipment to enable the company to manufacture this Polygon pipe, he borrowed $5,000 and took stock in the company for that amount. This development not only gave him a substantial interest in the company, it made him a partner instead of an employee.

Slowly, as he gained experience and confidence in himself, his relationship to Major Lloyd changed perceptibly. At first the Major had been interested chiefly in getting the best possible return out of what had seemed to be somewhat of a bad bargain, and had indicated he did not want to assume responsibility in the management of the business.

After his manager indicated sufficient faith to become a partner, the Major became very much interested in the whole adventure.

The two men began to discuss their mutual affairs more frankly.

One day the conversation touched on the possibility of better profits in the future. George said he thought they might be increased very easily, not in the future but immediately.

"How is that?" asked the Major. George replied, "I really feel that our rent is too high, considering the rents paid for other property in the neighborhood."

Major Lloyd stroked his whiskers as he studied the figures presented. Then he smiled, for *he* was the landlord! The facts presented were so sound that he then and there made a substantial reduction in the rent.

"Any other timely suggestions?" he asked. George replied (he was doing the smiling this time): "Considering that you have never wished to assume any responsibility in the conduct of the business, I really feel that the president's salary is also too high." That was a broadside, as the Major was the president.

It hit the mark. The Major laughed heartily and, slapping his daring young manager on the back, generously agreed to a reduction of his presidential salary. That was the beginning of better days for the roofing company.

This whole procedure was daring of a rather desperate sort, for George was a father now and therefore much less inclined to jeopardize his place in the company than he might have been earlier.

Shortly after the birth of his son Calvin on September 19, 1889, he had moved his family to a modest home he had built on Melrose Avenue in South Norwood, a new Cincinnati suburb which was then open country linked to the city only by rutted roads and a narrow-gauge railway. Though the family lived here three years, George Verity never rode on that railway. Since the day when Grandfather Deaton had lifted him onto the back of a horse, he had wanted to own a horse of his own at the earliest opportunity. He had accomplished that desire before moving to South Norwood; so, in fair weather, he rode horseback to work, some six miles, and in foul weather he used a buggy.

After his success in getting Major Lloyd to reduce both his salary and the rent, his position suddenly looked less secure than it had before. Unexpectedly he learned that the manager of a St. Louis plant in which the Major had an interest was urging consolidation of the several plants in which Major Lloyd was interested and was offering himself as president. The deal was apparently about to be closed when a fire broke out in the factory on the Public Landing, and the building was almost completely destroyed. The fire was followed by snow which further injured the exposed stock of sheet metal.

New quarters were promptly rented near the old, but in the meantime the proposed new general manager in St. Louis was summoned to assist in the planning and rebuilding. George, however, had moved so rapidly and effectively in procuring a new factory building and salvaging and restoring the injured machines, that by the time the gentleman from St. Louis arrived there was nothing for him to do. After a brief visit, he returned home.

After the proceeds of a fire sale of damaged materials were added to the insurance payments received, the company's financial status had improved to such an extent that George suggested a reorganization.

"Why should we continue to operate under the name of a company that failed?" he asked.

"Why, indeed?" said the Major, and the L. L. Sagendorph Iron Roofing & Corrugating Company became the American Steel Roofing Company, with George M. Verity as vice president and general manager.

The eighties ended, closing a chapter in the life of this preacher's son who had become, almost accidentally, an executive of a steel company. It was an ominous moment for a tyro to enter the steel industry, for that industry was becoming a jungle in which struggled reckless and ruthless men.

5

End of an Era

For the final decade of the nineteenth century there is a confusion of conflicting names. Better than the individual descriptive phrases, the confusion describes it. It was an era of explosive eruptions, a time when many things ended. Too, it was a time of many beginnings, the shape of whose ends is not clear even now, a half-century later.

Among nations and within nations the decade raised the question: Shall men co-operate or compete? In the United States the sun was setting on the exploitation of the most magnificent natural endowment ever offered any collection of humans. The westward-flowing wave of restless, freedom-seeking people, co-operators by compulsion of competitive environment, had struck the barrier of the Pacific and had now to recoil and settle. Great masses of capital, piled up as a result of this rapid conquest of a continent, had now to seek new worlds to conquer.

In the scramble for new conquests, competition between enterprisers became "cut-throat," and sorties into co-operation became sinister attempts to apply the strangle hold of monopoly. In the years after Appomattox, the favorite field for the freebooters of finance had been the railroads. As the century neared its end and railroad expansion neared its peak, banker John Pierpont Morgan silenced a protesting railroad president's complaint about "interference" with the blunt retort:

"Your roads? They are not your roads! They belong to my clients."

Order was now replacing chaos in railroading, and the rugged individualists who had mined pay-dirt in that chaos had to seek new claims to stake. Industry became their new bonanza.

In quantity and value of product, the United States had become the world's leading manufacturing nation. In a quarter of a century American enterprise had surpassed what had been accomplished magnificently and without precedent in a century in England. A billion invested dollars had become twelve billion. Employed wage-earners rose from 1,500,000 to 5,500,000. Value of products manufactured annually increased fifteen-fold.

All this had been done without much thought of whether it had been the fruit of co-operation or competition. But now the question was emerging and the issue was to be joined, for the four great provinces of business enterprise—the extractive, manufacturing, transport and financial processes—were being pulled together by increasing ties of federation.

Before the century ended, three-fourths of the nation's manufactures came from stockholder-owned factories; each large industry was a web of associated units and interlocked controls, and "trusts" were gaining controls of such staples as salt, sugar, meat, oil, whisky, copper, lead, coal, iron and steel.

In this final decade, the freebooting promoter, driven out of railroading, now invaded industry and tossed together collections of competing plants which were brought under co-operative

Jonathan and Mary Ann Verity between 1861 and 1865.

H. Allen Murray Studio

George Matthew and Jean Verity on their wedding day, October 19, 1887.

management. New securities were issued covering these consolidations and sold to the public. In the final year of the decade alone, there were incorporated new industrial companies with a total capitalization of $3,593,000,000, of which $2,354,000,000 was common stock.

In this era, the field which was especially tempting to such hydraulic financial engineering was the fabrication of iron and steel. From 1870 to 1890 the American output had grown from a trickle into a flood that constituted one-third of the world's annual output. In the nineties this industry, thriving as a result of the civilized world's insatiable hunger for things fabricated from iron and steel, was shaken again and again by the grasp of gamblers to whom competition was a thing of rending claw, and "co-operation" meant python hugs and cobra kisses.

And here was the tyro George Verity, entering this field at exactly this ominous moment.

The key question of the time hit him hard almost immediately. He found that competition among the manufacturers of sheet-metal building materials was excessively keen and that it was difficult to earn a fair profit no matter what the volume of business enjoyed. He was conditioned for this experience. From the time when, at fourteen, he had stood his ground against chastisement, he had determined that he could hold his place, whatever it happened to be, and would not let anyone push him out of it. But, while he fought his associated competitors to remain in the contest, he repeatedly told them he thought their conduct was unnecessarily suicidal. In time, with necessity as a constant urge, a Sheet Metal Roofing Association was formed in an effort to promulgate more co-operative methods.

In this association, as in so many similar federations originated in that decade, the members were to discover again and again that gentlemen's agreements fail for want of gentlemen. Eventually, after encountering many difficulties and failures, the members elected Verity secretary and treasurer of the Association. Though he was still an active competitor, this position put him in very close contact with each member of the Association. It gave him an opportunity to understand not only their policies and methods but also the underlying causes for their keen competition.

It was now 1893. Within the Association there was peace—or at least a truce. As secretary-treasurer, Verity studied his manufacturer associates and their methods and finally reached the conclusion that peace was not possible except under some closer and more binding co-operative arrangement.

He further concluded that, as far as his own company was concerned, its strength would have to be built upon the good will and co-operation of his working associates, such as Schueller, Hogan, Rambo and the rest. "I'll pin my faith to men," he said.

In 1893 he decided the time had come for him to meet some of the company's outlying customers, especially the progressive buyers who served the Great Plains farmers, whose hunger for iron and steel products seemed insatiable.

Though it meant a long absence from his family, now increased by the birth of daughter Leah, he looked forward to this trip as an opportunity to widen his horizons. The Columbian Exposition had opened in Chicago, and he planned to visit it on his way home. There was much at this fair he wanted to see—the great dynamos that set machinery humming at the touch of the plump forefinger of President Grover Cleveland on a golden telegraph key, the twelve one-thousand-horsepower generators and the quarter of a million electric lamps created and installed by George Westinghouse, and the gas-engine-powered carriage built by Carl Benz in Germany. On the day of his departure he was a boy again.

As the train left, Major Lloyd shouted, "Don't forget to report on that town named Lloyd we found on the map of Montana!"

A fortnight later, the Major received a letter, containing the report:

"Lloyd, Montana, is a building that raced past the car windows in a blur of telegraph poles."

The Major, whose good humor was always in evidence, was unable even to smile, for he had just sent a telegram notifying his young associate that his son Calvin was dangerously ill.

"Diphtheria," he muttered, "is no joke."

The telegram caught up with the child's father during his return trip. Dropping everything, he headed for home. A week later he arrived. Day and night he sat at his son's bedside, thinking often of the time, far away and long ago, when he, exactly Calvin's age, tossed in a fog of fever in the home of Grandfather and Grandmother Deaton while his own father sat at the bedside.

How long he sat he knew only after the crisis had passed and he looked at himself and found he had not removed the clothing he had been wearing when he arrived home.

Then he concluded that South Norwood was too far out in the country. The distance, six miles, requiring an hour and a quarter to drive or ride horseback, was too great for his family's safety.

As soon as the convalescing boy could be moved, he bundled them all off for a summer-long holiday, a happy return to Epworth Heights where, nine years ago, he had first met Jean.

Then and there, he said, he realized that, "although an important fact of life is the earning of a living, the most important fact of life is to live it."

The summer done, he moved his family back to Newport, Kentucky, into a spacious old house on Front Street, facing the placid sweep of the Ohio. From the front door of his home father Verity could see the factory, and from the front windows of the factory manager Verity could see his home. The trips between home and factory, as compared to the long drive in from the former country home, were brief and easy minutes, walking, riding or driving over the bridge. In that first winter the Ohio was placid enough; it froze from shore to shore and the Veritys and their neighbors skated across repeatedly.

But there was no singing about the "Beautiful Ohio" in the spring, for this ordinarily smooth band of friendly water, goaded by sudden thaws, turned overnight into a writhing, roaring, foam-flecked monster clawing at homes and factories along its banks.

This was George's introduction to floods, and floods were to be important in his career. This one drove him out of his home to a house on higher ground where a second daughter, Sara Genevra, was born.

Recurrent floods added excitement to the already sufficiently stimulated business on the Public Landing. They came with disastrous frequency. Whenever they threatened, the staff worked day and night, moving stock and some machinery to upper floors. Often the threat ended as such, and the labor was lost. Lost? Well, not entirely; for when men work together without thought of self in any soul-taxing struggle against a common foe there is a gain—a profit compounded of that deep understanding in which alone the seeds of good will find nourishment. It is a profit too elusive to audit, so the books of Will Rambo often reported these labors in the red ink of loss.

Red ink would be the proper medium for the recording of history in the months after the World's Fair of 1893. Before the year was over there was a stock-market collapse, followed by a succession of crashing banks. Then came a drain of gold toward Europe, followed by a downward plunge of silver value as a result of India's abandonment of bimetallism. As January of 1894 dawned, the United States government was virtually insolvent. A month later able-bodied men were eagerly exchanging a day's labor for a bowl of weak soup in Chicago. In April Jacob S. Coxey was leading his ragged "Army of the Commonweal of Christ" toward Washington. Then 200,000 coal miners struck. The federal government was reduced to the ridiculous position of petitioner of assistance from financiers. The people's indignation rose into that muttering which may so easily become the roar of revolt. The booming-organ oratory of silver-tongued William Jennings Bryan was heard in the West. Shrewd Marcus Alonzo Hanna ground cigars to bits and worked and planned with Governor William McKinley. Pullman workers struck and summoned Eugene Victor Debs to help them unionize. The strike flared into violence; men died violently at Chicago's Monon depot; cars burned in the Burlington yards; railroad men struck in sympathy; the Knights of Labor pondered a nation-wide strike; and federal troops were called out. The strike was broken but the fear of revolution deepened as the depression dragged on into 1895, when J. P. Morgan formed a syndicate to prop the nation's credit.

Then came a riotous presidential campaign, a short flurry of business activity after McKinley's election, and, once more, a downward spiral of depression into 1897. That year talk ended because hope seemed dead. Then, for reasons still obscure, came an unprecedented boom that roared into high gear in 1898.

George Verity had little opportunity to watch these fireworks. He was too deeply concerned with the grim task of hanging on to his business while the explosions shook his hold again and again; for, amid the ruins of American industry, bold and reckless men were on the prowl, seizing control of mills and factories, attempting to create a tight monopoly of the iron and steel business.

At this time he began to feel that his sphere of interests was too narrow to enable him to understand the significance of the sinister forces at work behind the scenes in the nation. Until now he had put all his energy into his job. He feared he was becoming a single-interest "grind" with a single-track mind. This, he now decided, he could not let himself become in a world growing daily more complex.

"If I knew more, perhaps I could do more—and do it more effectively," he said.

He was not alone. Other young businessmen in Cincinnati felt as he did. But there was not much they could do about expanding their horizons, for this was long before the advent of such fine associations of young dreamers as the Junior Chamber of Commerce. True, there were civic clubs in all American cities. They had begun as active enterprises but many of them had become what enterprises become when they are decadent—institutions. They were tombs wherein the dry bones of antiquated ideas could rattle meaninglessly above smugness comfortably cushioned in rump-polished club chairs. From such mausoleums of arthritic cerebration, "pushy young upstarts" were barred.

In the end, a small group of active minds organized their own Young Men's Business Club of Cincinnati. George became a member during the third year of the Club and at that time the young rebels numbered about sixty. They met once a month in the old Grand Hotel. They indulged in the usual horseplay of ebullient youth. They talked a lot. They dreamed more; for, being young, their minds were big to bursting with the fecundity of magnificent ideals of social and civic improvement. Young Davids they were, bravely setting out to aim their slingshots at the Goliaths of local political corruption, social stupidity, economic dry-rot.

"Before I joined that club I thought I was too busy to think about the problems of my neighbors," George said later. "After I joined it I saw that I was a part of the community and belonged to it. It was one of the most important moves I ever made. It showed me that I couldn't live by myself, sufficient unto myself."

In 1898, his second year of membership, he was nominated for the presidency of the club and was elected in a campaign in which the club membership rocketed to more than five hundred. The campaign slogan devised by his friends was "Vim—Vigor—Verity."

His father, who had not yet completely reconciled himself to his son's choice of a career, read a newspaper account of how George had been honored at the club's annual dinner, and wrote to say that he was proud of him.

On October 3, 1898, George replied:

> "Our year has been a great success. . . . I am still chairman of the building committee and when we turn over the new clubhouse to them, I will be done."

As 1898 was slipping into history he was once more forced to devote his full time to his business. Another price war had broken out among the members of the Sheet Metal Roofing Association. While these men, his competitors, were scuttling their agreements and ruining one another with vicious practices, they were appealing to him as secretary to help them end their suicidal conduct. As 1899 arrived, he saw the pressing need for full concentration on his own affairs, for the end of the century was bringing great and sweeping changes in the iron and steel industry. Dimly he sensed that the furious fight among the small fabricators of steel was but a minor action in a huge battle shaping up between powerful forces striving to control the entire steel industry, from the ore deposits in the earth to the little shops that served the public's mounting needs for things made of iron.

In the struggles of the mighty for control of steel at the century's end, many small mills and factories were trampled into extinction.

Small fabricators like the American Steel Roofing Company fashioned metal products, such as roofing, siding, eavetroughs and downspouts from flat iron or steel sheets which they bought from sheet-rolling mills. Other small manufacturers operated shops in which sheets were galvanized or tinned. Serving them were many small sheet-rolling mills whose owners bought their billets and bars from larger ironmongers and steelmakers. In most cases the producers of billets and bars were dependent on blast-furnace operators who bought ore and coke from still larger companies. Year by year the hand of Andrew Carnegie had reached deeper and deeper into this loosely knit structure, gaining control at strategic points and pulling loose ends together until almost the entire industry was at the mercy of the Carnegie colossus.

As the Carnegie profits increased geometrically and the small operators' fears of the Carnegie power multiplied in direct ratio, the stage was set for a number of daring men to try to wrest some of the profits and power from the hands of the little Scot. Roving the outer marches of the Carnegie empire were such men as John Warne Gates, and the daring brothers James and William H. Moore. Gates had acquired his sobriquet, "Bet-a-million," through his willingness to risk anything. Once he won twenty-eight thousand dollars in a few minutes, betting a thousand dollars each on the raindrops falling on a Pullman car window. Another time he coolly dropped a million dollars in another Pullman-car bet on the turn of one playing card.

Dreaming of himself as not only Carnegie's competitor but head of the world's first billion-dollar corporation, Gates was quietly buying up steel mills and factories and jockeying himself into a position of control in the larger companies that had survived the Carnegie competition. By 1898 he had gained virtual control of steel wire production as head of a merger of a score of properties. Through his boyhood friend, Elbert Henry Gary, he maneuvered himself into power in the Illinois Steel Company which, forged with those steel rails that Captain Ward was rolling when George Verity was born, had become Carnegie's chief but not dangerous rival.

Fired by the example of Gates's successes, other enterprisers succumbed to the merger mania. The Moore brothers, founders of Diamond Match and National Biscuit, turned their attention to steel and formed a syndicate with Daniel G. Reed and William B. Leeds which put 265 tin-plate mills together in the new Tin Plate Trust.

Once, in this time of monumental lunacy, a group of hard-boiled "captains of industry," while riding on a train, recalled there was a mill in the next town and, signaling a stop, spilled pell-mell out of their private coach into the mill-owner's house, rousted him out of bed and overrode his disinclination to sell his mill, which he valued at a hundred thousand dollars, by paying him half a million.

If a small operator refused to sell, a price war usually brought him around to a reasonable attitude.

Then, through his respect for Judge Gary and his dislike for Gates, Morgan was drawn into the war by the formation of Federal Steel Company, an amalgamation of the many companies which Gates had thrown together.

This issue was now being joined; the saurians of steel were getting set for battle. The public watched, uncertain whether to fear or cheer.

In his Fifth Avenue mansion, Carnegie watched. But not with uncertainty! He grinned in his beard. His company's profits had now climbed to the staggering total of $40,000,000 annually. He held all the aces and knew it. He also knew the time had come to make the final play, cash the chips and leave the game.

This incredible man, who had asserted all along that he cared nothing for money, was now preparing to demonstrate that he meant what he said—cannily planning to retire as America's richest man and devote the rest of his life to giving away his fabulous accumulation of personal wealth.

Early in 1899 he had quarreled with his partners Frick and Henry Phipps. Frick left, the companies were reorganized with Charles Michael Schwab as president, and plans were publicized for a huge expansion program, which threw the industry into panic. Carnegie announced he would compete with them all, and the frightened enterprisers flew to Morgan, begging him to buy out Carnegie and organize the whole steel industry into one huge combination.

There was a duck dinner in December, 1900, at which Morgan was seated next to the charming, smooth-tongued Charlie Schwab who, called upon to speak, rose to his feet and painted for the assembled steelmasters a colorful word-picture of the fair world of monopoly which might be theirs if—— After dinner Morgan and Schwab talked earnestly. A few days later, Morgan requested option terms on the Carnegie properties. Carnegie granted no option but scribbled his price on a slip of paper—$400,000,000 for his company. On March 2, 1901, the deal was closed and the birth of the United States Steel Corporation was announced. A month later, capitalization was raised to $1,100,000,000—a billion-dollar corporation dominating the world of iron and steel.

Hard and often the seismic upheavals in this period shook George Verity, both as vice president of his company and as officer-peacemaker in the Sheet Metal Roofing Association. For such associations Carnegie had a great contempt. "Bad business," he called them, "strengthening the other fellow as much as they strengthen you." What Carnegie knew instinctively, Verity had to learn through bitter experience.

Early in 1899, before Morgan began "tossing cats and dogs together and calling them elephants," the cats and dogs of this

Roofing Association were weary of battle once again and were calling for peacemaker Verity.

Neglecting his own business, he diligently worked out a plan for co-operative ownership and operation of all factories engaged in the manufacture of sheet-metal building materials. There were about twenty-five in the country. His plan proposed that each company turn its property and equipment into an operating company at an appraised valuation. The individual owners would receive stock in the operating company in proportion to the appraisals. Management of the operating company would be selected by stockholders from among members.

The plan proposed to reduce costs by consolidation of manufacture into four plants, situated strategically so as to effect savings in transportation costs and volume buying of materials. Individual factory buildings not used for manufacture were to be warehouses for sales distributors. As such they would buy finished products from the four fabricating plants at fixed prices.

His plan evolved from his own recollection of how Barney Kroger had effected savings in the marketing of groceries. Calling on the manufacturers, he told them:

"I'm convinced that the economies we can achieve in co-operative action through volume buying and condensed large-scale manufacture will enable us all to remain in business with reasonable profits and yet sell our products at much less than they have ever been sold."

His logic moved them. Options were obtained from virtually all of them. True, they were weary of economic cannibalism and frightened by the ruthlessness of the mergers then afoot, but they trusted him, and their trust in him was heartening as he labored day and night over the plans for financing and fought against a succession of delays and disappointments.

Finally, after assembling all the necessary facts and securing the needed options, he announced that $800,000 would be needed to pay cash for inventories of the member companies and to provide sufficient working capital. Major Lloyd, whose wife had died, was then living at the Verity home. Consulted, the Major proposed to take his associate to New York where he had friends and acquaintances who he felt assured could help raise the necessary funds.

Together they went to Manhattan and were well received by a financial firm which in the end agreed to underwrite the issue. This result was not, however, attained until much hard work had been done. The night the underwriting agreement was secured they retired, jubilant because a job had been well done. Next morning they learned their jubilation had been premature. During the night, Roswell P. Flower, former governor of New York and head of the nation's largest brokerage house, died and the stock market broke badly the next morning. With such a market the deal was off, at least temporarily, and they returned to Cincinnati, nursing their disappointment.

Back home once more, Verity plunged into his own business, deciding to leave peacemaking to others for the time being and pay strict attention to charting the course of his little company through these stormy times.

He had just pigeonholed the plan for co-operation, to concentrate again on competitive problems, when his office door opened and there stood before him a tall, well-dressed young man who introduced himself.

This young man said he had a plan which had been drawn up by his uncle, a Cambridge banker and former Ohio member of Congress, whom George had known well and whom he respected and admired.

It was no news to George when the young man explained that his uncle, the owner of a small sheet-metal fabricating plant, similar to that of the American Steel Roofing Company, had planned to build a mill to roll his own sheets.

"The plans," he added, "were completed before my uncle's death and are now in my possession. A small group, including my cousin, who lives in Washington, and myself have arranged to raise one-half the estimated $400,000 required to go forward with the plans, and I am now seeking a partner and a site for the mill.

"Because my uncle had such a high regard for you and your company, it occurred to me that you and your friends might like to join us by raising the other half of the needed funds, and taking an active interest in the business."

The proposal was interesting, especially when this prosperous-looking fellow presented evidence that he had already begun negotiations with officials of two cities, each of which would pay the company a substantial bonus and donate a site for the proposed mill. One of the cities was Zanesville, which offered a site on the Muskingum River, and the other was Middletown, with a site on the edge of town.

Coming on the heels of the disappointment in New York,

this proposal was very stimulating. Verity agreed to visit both cities and examine the proffered sites. At Zanesville he confirmed his new friend's claims that the city was willing to donate a site and that the Chamber of Commerce offered to pay a bonus of $75,000. In Middletown, the Industrial Commission, appointed by the mayor to bring new industries into the town, matched the Zanesville offers. As the ultimate choice was left to him, George went home to think.

A link with a rolling mill, he saw readily enough, would strengthen the fabricating business on the Public Landing. If he and his friends in the fabricating business held half-interest in such a mill they would have a protected source of supply in these times when sheet mills were being gobbled up by dominating mergers. A mill at Middletown, he decided, would be more advantageous than one in Zanesville, for Middletown was on the Miami Canal and the low cost of shipping sheets to Cincinnati would be a more important factor than the cheap fuel available in Zanesville.

So he informed the Middletown Industrial Commission that he would accept their offer if and when proposed plans were carried out. He then asked the promoter to produce his uncle's plans and estimates and disclose the names of his partners. The man pleaded for time. When, however, he continued to evade the requests with progressively weaker excuses, Verity wrote to the banker's son in Washington for the desired information.

The reply was most disconcerting. The letter said that Verity's new acquaintance was the black sheep of the family, and added that the writer had his late father's plans for building a sheet mill and would not surrender them to his cousin in any circumstances.

Swallowing the bitterness of his second successive disappointment and curbing his temper, Verity congratulated himself upon the fact that he had not as yet attempted to find associates in the venture and was therefore free to go ahead with it or drop it.

The more he thought of the plan, the more interesting it seemed.

"If I must, I'll try it alone," he said.

His first problem was to get rid of the black sheep. It proved to be a real problem, for the man brazenly claimed right of participation because he had secured offers of sites and bonuses, and for this he demanded a substantial amount of cash. As a last resort, Verity called on the fellow's brother, an able and respected official of a paper mill in near-by Lockland, and with his assistance the promoter was persuaded to sign a release of all personal interest on condition that he be paid $6,000 if and when either bonus offered was paid.

Two factors now drove Verity forward with this idea of a mill at Middletown: he saw the advantage of such a mill, and he felt he had made a promise to the people of that community and should do everything possible to work out the conditions of the promise even though no papers had as yet been signed.

"I have my tail so far under the gate," he said, "that I feel I must go ahead."

But he had no plans, no estimates. He didn't even know what kind of machinery and equipment a sheet mill actually required. He had no partners, and no liquid assets. All he had was a home in Newport, his stock interest in his company and his salary. His knowledge of what happened to iron and steel sheets before they came to his shop for conversion into building materials was very slight.

"Well," he said, "I'll have to learn."

So he called on a friend who was ten years his senior and who had been working in iron and steel since he was eighteen. This friend was kindly, roly-poly William Thomas Simpson whom George had known for ten years both as a personal friend and as a customer for his sheet iron.

Simpson knew mill processes. As a boy of fourteen he had earned his first pay as conductor on a coach line, and at eighteen had helped his father organize on Pearl Street the first galvanizing shop west of the Alleghenies. In 1890 he had bought the old Riverside rolling mill which had supplied his galvanizing plant with black iron sheets, and had organized the Cincinnati Rolling Mill Company. In 1897 he revamped his mill to produce tin plate instead of sheet iron and had reorganized as the Cincinnati Rolling Mill & Tin Plate Company. Then, in January, 1899, the Tin Plate Trust had bought him out.

Genial Will Simpson listened sympathetically as the younger man tumbled out his problem.

"Verity," he said at last, "that sounds like an interesting adventure and an opportunity to strengthen your manufacturing business."

After a decision was reached, Simpson introduced Verity to friends of his in Cincinnati and Pittsburgh and together they got pledges of subscriptions for about $350,000 for common stock if and when issued.

"The estimate of the cost of getting started is too low," said Simpson after further consideration. "You'll need at least $500,000."

Now Major Lloyd's interest was aroused and he promised to undertake the sale of $150,000 of preferred stock.

With these pledges in hand, Verity faced the problem of actually creating definite plans for a sheet mill. Until now there had not been a pencil mark on paper. Again Will Simpson was helpful, so helpful that George put him down for $2,500 in stock in the new company for his advice and assistance. The elder man introduced Verity to Isaac W. Frank of the United Engineering and Foundry Company, makers of rolling-mill equipment, and Frank took the tyro under his wing.

Off to Pittsburgh now he went to watch the fiery birth of the material he had been working with for more than a decade. He saw the ore come down from those northern deposits that were being discovered the day he was born. He watched it being wedded to coke in the blast furnaces, saw it flow out in an incandescent stream and become pig iron. He watched the birth of steel in the great Bessemer converters which were being introduced to America in the April of his birth. He watched the molten steel being poured into great ladles and the boiling content of the ladles being "teemed" into molds where it congealed and became ingots. He saw ingots squeezed into billets and bars in blooming mills and bar mills. And he stood spellbound as gigantic men, their rippling muscles reflecting fire-glow in the sweat-shine of straining backs, deftly but laboriously fed cherry-red bars into rolls which squeezed them into sheets. Such things he saw and was fascinated, as all men are who see them for the first time or the hundredth time.

Everywhere he asked questions, setting down the answers in his pocket notebook. Every night he retired to his hotel room and studied his notes. He had taken a surveyor's plat of the Middletown site with him. Day after day for four months he studied equipment and processes and discussed plans and ideas with Isaac Frank and anyone who could give him any needed information. Night after night he sat in his room quilting the ideas together on the surveyor's plat.

The original idea had been to have the new mill roll sheets from bars bought from a steel mill. At Pittsburgh, where the broader picture of the battle for control of steel production was more discernible, it became plain to him that his proposed plant would have to make at least part of its own steel to insure its independence. Otherwise he would still be at the mercy of the larger merging groups in the industry.

To make his own steel he would need a Bessemer converter. But he had to dismiss that thought when he learned that such a converter would cost more than the planned expenditure for the entire plant.

He and Simpson discussed this issue fully and decided they should investigate the new open-hearth process for making steel, which was just being introduced in some of the large plants of the country.

Though the open-hearth furnace was first tried in England

on a commercial scale in the year of Verity's birth, it was only now being introduced in the United States. Unlike the Bessemer converter which demanded specific kinds of ore as its diet, the Siemens-Martin furnace could convert pig iron and scrap iron into steel. True, it was slower in its production than the converter, but it was less expensive to build and required less skill to control. Most steelmakers had so far shunned it, largely because it was a novelty and because most of them were then trying to stave off revolutionary change; but one battery of the furnaces was then being erected in Birmingham and another was being built in Chicago.

When the Verity plans were finally pieced together on the surveyor's plat they called for a twenty-five-ton open-hearth furnace, the smallest practical unit. Planned also were four sheet mills, a bar mill to convert ingots into sheet bars, and a galvanizing department.

The plan to link an open-hearth furnace with a sheet mill was daring pioneering. It had not been done before. Had it not been done here, the subsequent research and development of invention, which proved to be the strength of the new company, could never have been begun.

Simpson backed Verity up in his suggestion that it should be tried and gave him the name of a young steelmaker he knew, who, he felt, could build and operate the furnace.

Now George Verity had a plan, a guarantee of a site and a bonus of $75,000 from Middletown, the promises of 35 men to subscribe $350,000 and Major Lloyd's promise to raise an additional $150,000 in the sale of preferred stock.

But about that time the Major decided to make a trip to Europe, and to do so he had to let his promise to raise $150,000 go by the boards.

"Gee whiz!" said Verity in telling this story in later years. "Was I in a mess!"

He was in a mess indeed. He had now entered into a contract with the city of Middletown to build a plant. The contract stipulated that as soon as the plant was in operation and providing a monthly pay roll of $25,000, the Commission would pay the promised $75,000. That sum was to be turned into the common-stock fund to reduce the price per share to the subscribers.

His state of mind at this time is revealed by a letter he wrote on a train to Pittsburgh, replying to his father's expression of concern over the magnitude of his undertaking.

> "Major was called to Europe and left me to work it out alone, but I have entered into a contract to build a mill and *it will be built.*"

The last four words were doubly underlined.

Speaking in the same letter of the difficulty of raising the necessary funds, he said his chief anxiety was "to secure good people who will not make us trouble in managing it."

The company was incorporated as the American Rolling Mill Company on December 2, 1899, with a tentative capital stock of $200,000. It was intended that capitalization would be increased to $500,000 before actual construction began. When the Major went to Europe, George turned again to his old friend

Will Simpson for advice. This time Simpson's aid was financial. A bond issue was substituted for the proposed preferred stock and Simpson and his brother Frank, both of whom later became directors of the company, took some of the bonds and sold the rest.

On March 17, 1900—St. Patrick's Day—capitalization was increased to $500,000, of which $350,000 was in common stock and $150,000 in bonds. There were 35 stockholders. George Verity was president and treasurer; William Simpson, vice president; Rufus Phillips, secretary.

The rough sketches, amateurishly put together in a Pittsburgh hotel room, were converted into blue-print plans by a Cincinnati architect, and the American Rolling Mill was ready to begin to build its proposed plants. Save for one detail, the Reverend Jonathan Verity's son was now ready to become a steelmaker.

That one detail—the most important in his eventual success—was *men.*

6

Men and a Mill

AGAIN, fate was kind to George Verity. Better, perhaps, than he knew sheet-mill practices, William Simpson knew sheet-mill practitioners, both the men and their characteristics. Then, as now, the workers in steel were bound together by strong ties of family and mill traditions and mutual interest in their survival.

Simpson knew how quickly the news of the Verity need for men would travel along that grapevine of information maintained by steel workers via correspondence and visits with "buddies" in distant mills.

Many men in the industry were then restless with a deep dissatisfaction arising from the widespread mergers and the resultant closing of mills. In every steel-mill town were excellent craftsmen, nursing grouches and ready to leap at a chance to work for an honorable independent employer. Verity met this need and opportunity by sending a representative to the steel towns to interview men who had lost their jobs through mergers. He offered employment to such men as he felt would best meet the need of the new company.

Soon, the industry's best men, coming from many places, converged on Middletown—the melters and helpers and ladlemen; the pitmen and gasmakers and skull-crackers; the riggers and fitters and cranemen; the rollers and heaters and catchers; the aristocrats of the crafts and the plain toilers.

They drifted in quietly to look things over and see for themselves whether the situation was such as had been pictured to them.

They had been told that the new boss admitted he knew nothing about the business. The candid confession pleased them. It inclined them to believe what he said when he declared that, surrounded by honest and able craftsmen, he hoped they would learn together, through day-by-day experience, how to solve their new and unfamiliar problems through co-operative effort.

This was a new line of talk to them. They looked around with eyes that had seen falsehood often and were not to be tricked again. They were seriously critical of all they saw. This mill, they saw, was a very small one even as mills went in those days. They heard of the proposal to bring together, for the first time, the processes for making steel and fabricating it into finished product. They could see the advantages of such a program; yet it was conceded to be an experiment. Could it hope to succeed?

Could such a small concern hope to survive in the face of the gigantic corporation then being formed? So they asked themselves if they should play safe and go along with the industrial giant that had taken over their several mills, or bet on the long odds and risk their future on this young pioneer who said:

"I'll pin my faith to men."

Some came, looked, listened—and left. They had heard fine talk before! Others remained—remained because an intangible something, felt seldom and seen never, spoke to that part of each man which longs for an opportunity for loyalty. Uncommonly large was the proportion who remained—yes, and for ten, twenty, thirty, forty years.

On July 12, 1900, the people of Middletown marched in a parade. The town was getting a new industry—and it needed it!

For by 1900 Middletown had stopped growing. To brave pioneer Daniel Doty it had shown great promise in 1792, when he staked his claim on this hill-girdled flood plain of the Great Miami's east bank and returned to New Jersey to fetch family and friends to the rich valley. Great, too, was its promise to Stephen Vail and James Sutton who platted the village in 1802 and called it Middletown because it was midway up the section of the river then navigable to the "Kentuck" flatboats. The promise enlarged in 1825, when DeWitt Clinton there gave the signal to start digging the Miami Canal. By 1833, when the canal was alive with packets, the city was incorporated and had become a teeming market center. Farmers, driving thousands of hogs to this busy port for shipment to Cincinnati, called it "Porkopolis." A thousand people passed through the community every week on the busy waterway.

Then the railroads came. In 1852 the Cincinnati, Hamilton & Dayton Railroad (now part of the Baltimore & Ohio system) linked it to Cincinnati and the South and to Toledo and the North. Twenty years later the Big Four Railroad joined it to Columbus and Cleveland. The nation's pork-packing center moved to Chicago, the valley farmers shifted from hogs to tobacco, and the town became one of the largest producers of chewing tobacco. As the railroads diminished the canal's traffic, Middletonians impounded the surplus water and set up the first of many paper mills which made the community an important center for paper-making.

Despite these adaptations to change, the growth of the town had slackened by 1900, when the population was about nine thousand, and the mayor had empowered the Industrial Commission to spend $100,000 if necessary to bring in additional industry.

So, on this July morning, Middletonians were in a mood to celebrate the resurrection of promise. The mill, they had heard, would employ 350. It was something to cheer about. Stores closed, the militia turned out, and the streets were festooned with bunting. After a ceremony at the City Hall, the crowd strung itself out in a parade that moved along the horse-car line on Third Street (now Central Avenue) and, turning down Curtis Street, kicked up the dust of that country road as the blaring brasses, thumping drums and flapping banners moved toward Doty's Grove.

Across the road from the grove was the twelve-acre site of the mill. Part of the original settler's grant, it bordered land occupied by the Daniel Doty homestead, a house that was later converted into a club for mill employees.

On arrival at the grove, Middletonians uncovered while the Reverend Rufus W. Weaver, pastor of the Baptist Church, invoked a blessing on the enterprise. City solicitor W. S.

Harlan then welcomed "the gentlemen of the American Rolling Mill Company" with a speech that compared their fortitude and daring to nothing less than "that energy and courage that is even now contemplating the construction of the great Nicaraguan Canal." Then he pulled out the diapason for "this great enterprise . . . this plant of such mammoth proportions."

Tall talk, that, for the welcoming of a little mill planned at a moment when Morgan and Gary were moving toward the launching of a billion-dollar steelmaking corporation!

But there was one passage in the speech in which the solicitor was a good prophet. Said he:

"May there ever exist harmony between employer and employee!"

Responding to the welcome, George Verity thanked the city officials, confessed pride in launching the first steel manufacturing plant in this part of the United States, and reiterated Harlan's hope that here steel would be made without strife.

There were more speeches, a cornerstone-laying and a flag-raising, all signalizing the birth of an organization that came to be called ARMCO.

The crowd dispersed and the dust settled. George Verity accompanied his family to the train that was to take them back home to Newport. With them went Major Lloyd, Simpson, Phillips and other friends. Returning alone to his room at Middletown's United States Hotel, he thought of the strange twists his life had taken lately. It was as if he had read all this as having happened to someone else. Only a short while ago, believing he would always live in Cincinnati, he had finally bought that Newport home in which his family had lived as tenants for years. Until almost yesterday he had thought of this Middletown mill as an adjunct to his Cincinnati plant, yet now it had been decided to bring the fabricating machinery here as soon as the mill was finished and combine the whole business under one group of roofs.

Would this little plant of his survive the blighting frost of grim realities then on the horizon? Just a week before, the Democratic National Convention in Kansas City had nominated Bryan for the presidency. The prospects for the re-election of McKinley, who had been called the "father of the tin-plate industry" in the previous campaign, looked none too bright. What sort of upheaval would the election of Bryan bring to the steel industry? What next? Troubling his mind that night was a mental image of himself standing on the brink of an abysmal unknown—a man desperately in need of the loyalty, faith and co-operation of many men.

Hands he needed; many hands with many skills; hands coupled to independent and ingenious minds; hands and minds implemented by stout hearts with large capacities of that mountain-moving faith which men so lavishly bestow upon a leader gifted with the knack of rendering them capable of deeds which they could not undertake alone.

"I *must* pin my faith to men," he said.

The men came.

First came Robert Brown Carnahan, Jr., whom Simpson had recommended to build and operate the open-hearth furnace.

Born in 1869, graduated from the University of Pittsburgh in 1891, Bob Carnahan began a brilliant career in metallurgy with research in gold-refining processes. In 1893 steel lured him from gold and his sharp mind focused on the then new open-hearth process of steelmaking. He supervised the building of the first furnace in Birmingham, and in 1899 was called to Carnegie's Homestead Works to apply his knowledge there. There was a bright future for him in the Carnegie company, for its reorganization was then thrusting many of the young partners up into key positions from which they were to step a year later as "Pittsburgh millionaires."

But when his friend Simpson told him of the Verity plan to link an open-hearth furnace to a bar mill, four sheet mills, a galvanizing shop and a fabricating plant in a continuous chain under one roof, he could not resist the opportunity to take part in that pioneering. Thus he became Armco's first employee.

Next came James B. Strawbridge, a quiet, studious and cultured Philadelphian. Experienced in the steel business, he was made general superintendent.

From Pittsburgh came burly Tom Rogers with a steelworker's tan upon his hard-bitten features; a man unlettered but exceptionally well versed in the hornyhanded art of rolling sheet metal.

These three came while construction was in progress. Each bought a small block of stock. Together they constituted George Verity's first board of strategy.

When construction began in the spring of 1900, many men had been hired. Many were proud masters of steelmaking crafts who left good positions to come here and take part in the construction work so as to be on hand when the furnace blew in and the rolls began turning.

As the year drew to a close Secretary Phillips and such of the Cincinnati staff as were willing came to Middletown with the machinery and equipment of the old factory. Simpson transferred William R. Price to the Armco staff to handle the employment and keep the time of the men who were now coming in from all parts of the country.

In all, there were about two hundred employed when the furnace was ready at January's end.

In the morning of February 7, 1901, after all the men had fidgeted through thirteen hours of apprehensive expectancy, Carnahan gave the order: "Tap the heat!" The melter yelled his *"Heow!"*—the signal for his helpers, the ladlemen and the pitmen to take their positions in preparation for the dreadful birth of steel. Swathed in wet burlap, helper Floyd Barlow moved along the catwalk behind and below the furnace, approached the taphole, knocked out the stopper and leaped nimbly aside as the roaring, seething Niagara of liquid metal gushed forth, spilling amid a cascade of rolling stars into the ladle handled by Orley Moles.

"The first baby was born" between midnight and dawn. In the fierce and hellish light of its birth, steel always dwarfs the attendant men to midgets who cast weird Dantesque shadows that dance grotesquely against walls. The shadows danced with uncommon liveliness this night, for there was great jubilation among George Verity's Cincinnati friends who had come to stand beside him and wait for this gorgeous spectacle of hell-blowing and fire-pouring.

It was a perfect heat, and some of it was molded into forms which, polished and nickel-plated, were inscribed with a memorial of the event and distributed among those who watched that night.

Two weeks later, on February 21, the first sheet of steel made from this heat emerged at the end of the roll train; and, at the month's end, when the first sheets had been galvanized and fashioned into finished products, the men of the little mill could boast that they had participated in the world's first conversion of pig and scrap iron into finished building materials in one continuous operation.

Now salesman Phillips could tell the customers: "We make our own steel and because we control its quality, we can guarantee a better finished product."

It was a practice weighted with so much natural advantage that other, larger steel companies subsequently adopted it. It is almost poetically ironic that on March 3rd, the very day the innovation became effective, the incorporation of the United States Steel Corporation was announced—and *that,* unpredictably, provided George Verity with exactly the men he needed.

By 1901, the people of America were embittered against corporate bigness by the growing abuses of monopoly. The public attitude toward conditions then prevailing expressed itself in the tremendous popularity of Edwin Markham's poem, "The Man With the Hoe," with its eloquent plea for more justice in

R. C. Phillips in office of Sagendorph Roofing Company.

G. M. Verity and R. C. Phillips near the turn of the century.

George Matthew Verity at the time of the formation of the American Rolling Mill Company, about 1900.

the distribution of the fruit of man's labors. The public clamor for reform was the main issue in the presidential campaign of 1900. That the popular Bryan failed to make capital of the public mood was due only to the even greater popularity of his opponent's running mate, Theodore Roosevelt, whose appeal as the "hero of San Juan Hill" was turned on for McKinley.

Viewed retrospectively, events of 1901 seem almost master-planned steps toward reform.

In January, 1901, *Life* published this joke:

> "Who made the world, Charles?"
>
> "God made the world in 4004 B. C., but it was reorganized in 1901 by James J. Hill, J. Pierpont Morgan, and John D. Rockefeller."

Greatest of the trusts at that moment was the Rockefeller control of oil; yet, on January 10, Spindletop, the world's greatest gusher, came in and shortly afterward it became plain that absolute control of *all* petroleum was far from the grasp of any one group.

Though Morgan and Hill seemed to have the nation's railroad under control when *Life* indulged in its jest, by the following May 9 the Northern Pacific panic, resulting from Edward H. Harriman's raid on the Morgan-Hill stronghold, demonstrated that monopoly was far from absolute in railroads.

At the moment when the dread "steel monopoly" was born, the political enemies of Theodore Roosevelt were congratulating themselves for having shelved the "rabid reformer" in the innocuous vice-presidency. Six months later the anarchist Leon

Czolgosz's pistol shots in Buffalo knocked reformer Roosevelt off the shelf and the "Trust-buster" began to shake "the big stick" at "malefactors of great wealth."

Roosevelt's strength lay in the public's aversion for corporate bigness, the mood which was definitely beneficial to the little company in Middletown. How much the company benefited by this state of mind cannot be estimated. In one respect, however, benefits can be measured; for, shortly after the United States Steel Corporation was formed, the Amalgamated Association of Iron, Steel and Tin Workers of North America voted a strike in the corporation's mills. While this strike was in effect there was a dearth of sheet metal, which brought the Middletown mill a windfall of precious orders; and a fresh wave of highly skilled workers—some of the best in the business—came to George Verity and added their services to the company's assets.

Before long the working personnel had increased to some 350, and every last one of them had a lot of faith in this man. They had to have! Neither auditor nor banker would have given this new mill so much as a nod of encouragement in its infancy. There was not enough working capital. Time and again, young Chalmers Todd, the office boy, camped at the post office awaiting some customer's check which might enable the company to make a payment on a bill, effect the release of material held by the railroad or meet a pay roll.

There was not enough equipment, and, because the plant was revolutionary in its co-ordination of continuous processes, a breakdown on one machine or a lack of replacement parts often meant expensive delays. Not infrequently it meant complete shut-downs.

There were times when the breaking of one piece of equipment was the signal for virtually all the crews to knock off and go fishing. Other times men patched the damaged parts as best they could. John Hogan was a wizard at that. He patched the secondhand but sturdy old engine brought up from Cincinnati until it was a proud boast in the mill that the only original part of John's engine was the nameplate.

And there were times when there were liens against every pile of steel ingots in the yards.

There was no attempt to hide these facts from the men. Regularly, George Verity walked through the mill and the men could see by the slope of his shoulders that he was burdened. They were often called together and fully informed as to the company's many difficult problems.

Many of them admitted years later that they kept their ears to the steel "grapevine," listening for news of other jobs but hoping they would be able to stay here.

In time they learned that John Hogan's greasy little cubbyhole of an office was the place to watch for storm signals, as he was George Verity's most loyal supporter.

The salty, good-humored wisdom of the sympathetic Celt was always balm to the troubled presidential mind. Once, when the company was in extremely dire straits, John quietly went to the bank and offered to transfer his life's savings to the Verity account. The story of Hogan's faith became a legend with which to define that indefinable something the men came to call "Armco Spirit."

On many a night in these early years, George Verity, though exhausted to the breaking point, would spring out of sleep and listen for the telltale rumble which is the thunder-throated purr of a steel mill at work in the distance. If the night was silent, he leaped out of bed, dressed and hastened to the plant, either on horseback or in a buggy.

Yes, men had to have stout faith.

And stout backs!

In those days industry, by and large, was virtually devoid of labor-saving devices. Workers were still referred to as "hands," and with good reason.

In this open-hearth department, for instance, hands loaded the stock (pig iron and scrap) onto heavy, railroad-wheeled vehicles called "buggies"; hands and legs and straining backs pushed stock-laden buggies in front of furnace doors; hands opened the doors which were not then water-cooled; and hands pushed the stock into the furnace with heavy "charging peels," which were no tools for weaklings.

The furnace, burning producer gas, had two gas ports and one air port at each end; and for the continuous and intermittent reversal of gas and air required to build up the temperature of the incandescent "bath" of molten steel in the furnace, hands operated valves which are nowadays operated automatically. Since water-cooling jackets for furnaces had not then been devised, and since the space provided for cleaning slag pockets and the checker chambers beneath the furnace was inadequate and unbearably hot, the cleaning processes were hand tasks called "man-killers."

The charging level of this furnace was on the yard level and the checker chambers were underground. After simmering in the furnace for twelve or more hours, the twenty-five-ton batch of iron brew was tapped into a ladle, dropped into a pit and held under the spout by a thirty-ton crane. The pit also held that smaller ladle called "thimble" into which the slag of each heat was skimmed.

In this melting department, which was so low-roofed and poorly ventilated that men suffered much from terrific heat and stifling fumes, the melter was king for his "turn" or shift, and Carnahan was boss of the kings.

After he built that furnace, Bob Carnahan actually lived with it and its successors, sleeping on a cot in the company office and eating many of his meals in the plant. He seldom missed the tapping of a heat—an event which he, a quixotic blend of deep tenderness and profane gruffness, likened to the birth of a child. From the restless questing of this man's mind came much of the pioneering spirit which fired the company in its infancy and kept it in the van of research in steelmaking.

Like the first, the second and third heats were perfect. But when the fourth was ready to be tapped, the ladle crane broke down, and for twelve hours, while the riggers toiled amid the heat and the fumes near the ceiling, trying to repair the crane, the melter kept the bath boiling, only to have to trickle it out finally on the ground in a stream so thin that the resultant steel could be broken up with sledges and chisels and thrown on the scrap heap. Meantime, the excessive duration of high temperature buckled up the entire bottom of the furnace, and before the steel and slag remaining inside could be removed, a hole had to be dug by hand through concrete and steel more than a foot below the taphole.

Time and again the taphole "froze" full of congealed steel. These steel plugs, called "monkeys," are burned out easily nowadays with oxygen, but then they were either chiseled out by hand or burned out with a charge of twenty to thirty thousand pounds of pig iron which was a total loss at the end of the procedure.

At the end of the fortieth heat, the furnace was so badly burned that its roof caved in, and the bricklayers and laborers got their first taste of the fearsome task of repairing a roof with a boiling caldron of molten steel just below them. And that heat also was a total loss.

Besides the open hearth, there were bar-mill, sheet-mill and annealing furnaces, all operating on producer gas. The stationary gas producers were hand-poked and hand-fed. The gas house was always so full of fumes that the men were perpetually drowsy. One of the regular duties of first helpers was to keep gasmakers "awake," to use the simple word of a time before men understood the symptoms of anoxia.

Once past the pouring spout and in the ladle, the brew was in the care of the ladleman. It was that craftsman's duty to get the metal into the ingot molds. Here, too, hands worked at hazardous tasks now done safely by electrical machinery. The ladle was carried by crane over a group of iron molds, each eight by ten inches in cross section, so arranged that when steel was "teemed" (poured) from the ladle-bottom down through a central fountain, it flowed by gravity through tile runners beneath the molds and rose up in them. Work in this pouring pit was difficult and dangerous. Each ingot weighed between eight hundred and a thousand pounds. Ponderous then, they would be considered mere sash weights in today's mills. To strip them out of the molds after they solidified, men laid boards across their red-hot tops, wrapped themselves in wet burlap and walked out on the burning boards while they grasped chains dangling from the crane.

The chains were hooked into lugs at the top of a mold and the crane operator was given orders to lift. The stripper made his way back to the pit bank as best he could. After all the ingots on the bank side were stripped, the stripper, soaked with water before each trip, had to dart among the standing red-hot ingots and hook the chains to the remaining molds. That done, he had to dart in again and loop the chains around groups of ingots so that the crane could lift them and bear them to the cleaning floor. Burns were serious and frequent here. There were several bad accidents when ingots fell over.

At the cleaning floor, the tile runners or "sprues" were knocked off the ingots which were then borne by hand to the bar-mill furnace where they were "soaked" with additional heat. Soaking was another back-breaking task, for the ingots had to be turned over and over continuously to soak them evenly and the turning was done by tongs in men's hands.

Tongs, manipulated by hands but aided by an overhead trolley, bore the ingots to the roughing mill where each eight-by-ten-inch ingot was "given four passes" (thrust four times) through the rolls and so lengthened into a four-by-seven-inch billet. Thence by hands again to the finishing rolls where eight passes reduced it to a bar of a specified thickness, seven inches wide and from twenty-five to sixty feet long.

Sheared into desired sheet-bar lengths, the bar sections moved by hand to the sheet mill in which only the most powerful men could work at the many tasks requiring great strength, fine skill and almost superhuman endurance.

Only when you compare the back-breaking and hazardous tasks of that time with the mechanized and relatively safe methods employed in modern steel plants, do you realize the reasons for George Verity's deep faith in the power of human loyalties.

Not all of his early associates shared his faith, however.

7

Pursuit of Happiness

AS SOON as the men were assembled and the mill was operating, George Verity applied himself to the job of bringing about a better understanding of their problems and policies, to the end that a spirit of confidence and good will might be developed.

In the spring of 1902, he had worked and worried himself into a state of collapse. A serious digestive ailment, probably brought on by nervous tension, laid him low by robbing him of thirty pounds in a week. Physicians, despairing of keeping him quiet in Middletown, ordered him to take a rest at French Lick, Indiana, where he recovered. Thereafter for many years his life was regimented with strict diet and a prescribed schedule of work and rest.

His favorite recreation was his horseback ride from five to six o'clock every morning. He kept up his morning rides in season and out of season for many years, as he had no time for any other form of recreation.

Because of his lack of practical experience, he had set up his "board of strategy"—Carnahan, Strawbridge and Rogers—to help him manage this adventure, which in those days they called a continuous mill. The method was right. Of that he was certain. But his group of mill managers as a whole did not turn out to be the right men. Nothing wrong with Carnahan! No, he was an indefatigable and ingenious worker, and he continued to live in the mill office where he could be on the job night and day. Strawbridge, however, became fainthearted soon after the mill was in full operation. Verity learned that he was making pessimistic statements both to men in the mill and to business men in the community.

And Tom Rogers! There was perhaps no better sheet-mill man in the business than Tom. But he had been trained in the roughshod school of hire-and-fire management. He could not for the life of him comprehend the Verity faith in the value of understanding between men and management. It was impossible for him to treat men as Verity wanted them treated. Mill management, to Tom, was no riddle, but a simple process of trial and error. You hired a man and gave him a trial. If he failed, you fired him. That was, in his experience, the tried and true method, and co-operation was to him simply another word for "coddling." So it became more and more impossible for Tom to do things as the management wanted them done. He favored the old way.

Because of his honesty, hard work and long experience, Verity tried to reason with him.

"Can't you see, Tom," he said, "that your 'old way' doesn't make men want to do their best, and that it is therefore a wasteful way—a luxury we can't afford here?"

Tom would listen and seem to agree but he could not change his ways. Because he had bought stock in the company, he had a fixed belief he could not be fired and he continued in the error until the inevitable actually happened.

As it became more obvious that neither Rogers nor Strawbridge could be made to fit into the Verity plan of industrial democracy, George confided to Simpson that he must find a man with sufficient vision to see how necessary it was to the success of the company to have all employees feel that they were part of one group with a common interest.

"I'd like a young, energetic and ambitious man, if possible," he said. "Preferably, I'd like one not hardened in the old school."

"I think I know the man for you," Simpson replied.

Now the Verity destiny was to be affected by a man who at that time knew nothing of this new company and its problems.

This man—who was at that time unaware of the existence of George Verity—was a bearded Englishman named W. P. Lewis, who was reputed to have few superiors in the art of making sheet steel and tin plate. Born in 1866 in Gloucestershire, he learned his craft from his powerful father, Bill Lewis, the only man in England whom the great prizefighter, Tom Sayers, refused to meet in bare-knuckle combat. Young Lewis lived in England until he was twenty-two, working in mills in Lydney and Aberdair. Then he went to Millingriffith, Wales, and then to a mill in Bilboa, Spain. In 1898 he came to America at the urging of his boyhood friend, Charles Hillman, who later became an Armco roller but was at that time employed in Simpson's Riverside mill.

Lewis was a kindly man who took an interest in the young men who came under his supervision from time to time. As a class, English mill men were clannish to the point of considering it heresy to teach their crafts to strangers. Roll-turning, the secret of sheet-rolling, was particularly guarded by those who had mastered this art of shaping rolls.

When he was superintendent of the Riverside mill, Lewis became acquainted with Simpson's office boy, who seemed unusually ambitious and anxious to learn the business. This young man made such an impression on Lewis that he was permitted to come to the mill on Sunday, when it was closed, to learn the secret art of roll-turning under Lewis.

This former office boy, Charles Ruffin Hook, ultimately proved to be the "young man with vision" whom Verity had been seeking.

Charlie Hook was born in Cincinnati on July 12, 1880. The son of a carriage-maker, he went to work in the Riverside mill after he had graduated from Walnut Hills High School, and was more than a little dissatisfied with his prospects as a two-dollar-a-week office boy when Lewis offered to teach him "a real trade."

Just as he was rounding out this roll-turning experience, the new Trust bought the mill and sent him to its Chicago office as a clerk. In a few months he was moved to the New York office as an apprentice accountant. When he asked to be transferred to a mill where he could learn the business, his superiors thought he was daffy to ask for a demotion, but, granting his request, transferred him to their Morewood mill in Gas City, Indiana, as clerk to the superintendent, who turned out to be his old friend Lewis, the Englishman.

Under the wing of his friend once more, young Hook resumed his lessons, covering a much broader field of operations.

Young Hook picked up sheet-mill practice so quickly that he was made foreman in 1902, though he was only twenty-two and, being small and slight, looked at least five years younger. He was, indeed, so boyish in appearance that Verity was startled when Simpson introduced him.

Charlie Hook was a good listener, and Verity was soon deep in a discussion of his dreams and plans. He told him what kind of organization he was trying to create and outlined the company policies he was endeavoring to develop; explained how it all began, what he was up against, what his hopes and problems and policies were, and where the company's most serious weaknesses appeared to be.

"I firmly believe," he said, "that our present weaknesses can be converted into our main source of strength if all the men in our organization can be made to realize that it is to our mutual interest to work together and try to understand one another's problems.

"In fact our only hope for survival in competition with our large and well-financed competitors, as I see it, lies in our ability to build up a real spirit of co-operation between our management and our men. We cannot afford the wasteful hire-and-fire labor policies common to the industry. We *must* consider our men as co-workers, keep them fully informed of our problems and our policies and provide them with every sound incentive we possibly can. If we can do these things, we will not only hold our place in the industry but do a better job for our customers than any other mill in the country."

Young Hook listened attentively. He did not hesitate long in deciding to identify himself with this experiment.

Two things weighed heavily in his decision, he later recalled. One was the thought that participation in the success of this small company would be far more interesting than routine advancement in the Trust. The other was his belief, distilled from his own contacts with labor, that the idea of more humane management, here being forced into fruition by circumstances and by George Verity's determination to make it work, was one of those obvious truths so often and so strangely overlooked.

"I like your theories," he said. "I'll come."

On November 1, 1902, he was employed as night superintendent at $100 a month.

"Who's the kid?" said the former Tom Rogers millmen when they first laid eyes on him, for he was so slight and boyish that even Verity's associates in the management doubted the wisdom of hiring him for such an important post. In an attempt to allay these expressed fears, Verity had to request the young fellow to stop wearing such a boyish cap in the mill.

In taking on the responsibility of superintending the work of some of the industry's most capable veterans, young Hook was in about the same position that George Verity had been in when he came to the Standish store. Though these hard-shelled steelmakers laughed uproariously at some of the questions he asked, they grew to like him because he asked, not out of idle curiosity, but with a real desire to learn their problems. He carried a little notebook in which he set down what they told him. They found it was easy to make suggestions to him, that he was always willing to try something new or different.

One night, for instance, he came to Charlie Greer, a veteran who had come to Middletown because he didn't like working for the Tin Plate Trust. Charlie had just sheared a cambered or curved sheet. Hook pointed out its imperfection. At that time the management had an agreement with the local lodge of the Amalgamated Association of Iron, Steel and Tin Workers of North America; under its terms a workman was paid tonnage rates on that operation for every sheet whose width was the same at both ends and in the middle, if the ends were properly squared. Such measurements would be correct even when a sheet was cambered, or so shaped that it was a segment of a circle. Greer had tossed such a sheet on the stock pile.

"That's not a good sheet," said Hook.

Greer, saying nothing, applied his width gauge, showed that the measurements were right, and silently demonstrated that the corners were square. Straightening up, he asked:

"What's wrong with it?"

"I don't know what's wrong with it, Charlie," said Hook, "but you do, and you and I both know it's not a sheet that can be sold. What *is* wrong with it?"

Greer explained that camber was caused by some mill having unequal draft or pressure on the two ends of its rolls.

"That's just what I wanted to know!" said Hook. "Thanks, Charlie!" Walking away, he wrote furiously in his notebook. There were fewer cambered sheets after that.

Under the union rules men were also paid for laminated sheets even though such sheets were useless. The men knew the rule was unfair, but nothing was done about changing it.

One night Hook called them all off their jobs and marched them to the warehouse where he showed them a huge stack of the useless sheets for which they had been paid.

"Boys," he said, "if that stack gets big enough, the company will go broke and we'll all be out in the street looking for jobs."

Before the week was over, the Amalgamated lodge held a meeting and changed the rule.

On another night Hook was sitting in the office of the factory foreman, William P. DuChemin, when a man ran into the office and shouted that a mill had rolled a collar. A collar is a strip of hot steel that curls back and wraps itself around the rolls. It can cause a lot of damage in a split second. When Billy DuChemin heard "Collar!" he leaped from his chair as if shot out of it, and started for the door. But Hook, his chair tilted back, went right along with his interrupted sentence as if he hadn't heard the shout. Then, when he was finished, he said:

"Let's have a look at that collar."

Billy started to run, but Hook walked slowly, as if out for a Sunday stroll. Reaching the collared mill, he gave orders just as if there were no cause at all for excitement. In a few minutes everything was cleared up, the mill was rolling again, and the two men were back in Billy's office.

"Charlie," said Billy, "how can you keep as cool as that under such conditions?"

"Billy," replied Hook, "did you notice that everybody knew exactly what to do when we reached the mill?"

"Yes, but——"

"Well, I was probably the only one who didn't know what to do, so I walked slowly and tried to think. When I reached the mill I still didn't know what to do, but everybody else who had seen me walk slowly thought I knew, and all of them had calmed down enough to think straight."

Thus, little by little, Charlie Hook learned and, learning, won the respect of the men. They soon stopped calling him "the kid" and were calling him Charlie.

George Verity knew he had chosen wisely when he learned that young Hook had been setting aside twenty-five dollars out of each month's salary for investment in the company's stock. As a stockholder he early espoused the then heretical doctrine which he later summarized in his favorite phrase:

"Take the mystery out of business."

Before Charlie Hook demonstrated his ability to carry out the Verity policies in the mill, the presidential problems had increased to such an extent that Verity had to seek some form of recreation that would engross his mind. Thus it came about that he bought an automobile, the first one to appear in Middletown. This curved-dash Oldsmobile, with its unpredictable quirks, would, he hoped, provide the recreation prescribed by his doctors.

It did—for a while.

But before the year was out, his busy mind was casting around for some other outlet for his restless spirit.

Actual operations of the plant were no longer his sole concern. "Finding Charlie Hook," he told his associates, "was like acquiring an additional right arm." Hook's mind complemented his own to such an extent that he was now able to devote all his efforts to the management and expansion of the business.

All his efforts? Well, not quite all.

Talking to the workmen in the mill, giving them "lifts" in his buggy or his automobile on their way to the shop or their homes, and meeting their families, he began to think of means whereby he might be able to assist in the improvement of living conditions in the community. He was a member of this community now, having moved his family into an old house he had bought at 230 South Main Street.

This house, the only residence available, had a pretentious front, embellished with a stone lion and sculptured decoration fit for a Medicean palace but disguising an interior that had decayed into deplorable disrepair.

An old house rebuilt for a local banker, it had passed to a banking creditor in Pennsylvania when its owner failed in business. Its price was so cheap and the terms were so reasonable that Verity bought it and set about the task of remodeling it.

"It's sure a mess, ain't it, Mr. Verity?" said Charlie Deiss, the mill electrician who had been called in to rewire it.

This house—a fine front hiding a disintegrating interior—was not unlike some of the school buildings and other institutions in the then small and undeveloped city, Verity discovered. The first need his family faced was the education of the children, Calvin, Leah and Sara.

After they were enrolled in old South School, their father soon learned about the school's shortcomings. All the grades and the high school, he discovered, were packed into one old, meagerly equipped building, and classes were conducted by woefully underpaid and overworked teachers.

As soon as Calvin finished eighth-grade studies, his father sent him to Cincinnati's Franklin School. Later, Leah was sent to Bartholomew School in Cincinnati and then to the Bennett School in Millbrook, New York. Sara went directly from Middletown grades to Bennett.

Thus one father was able to solve the problem of educating his children. But, he asked himself, what of his neighbors who were unable to obtain such advantages? The situation, he saw clearly, was scarcely conducive to the building of the kind of community spirit that he was striving for in his infant company.

"This sort of thing," he said, "breeds class distinctions, of which there are too many already."

Among his new neighbors he inquired about the possibility of correcting conditions. They replied that conditions were much worse than he suspected.

"But," they added, "it's useless to suggest changes, for when any one group tries to improve the school system, all the political factions scrap their differences and band together to defeat the proposal."

Then Verity met David E. Harlan who had just come to

Middletown to operate a paper mill. At that moment, Harlan was full to bursting with indignation over his discovery of a common practice which he called slavery.

"I find," said Harlan, "that it's custom around here for businessmen to take boys and girls out of school and put them to work without pay on the grounds that the kids are thus being educated. I think it's a rotten custom."

Verity agreed, and the two newcomers set out to discover the reasons for the custom. They learned that, while political factions and so-called reformers were constantly at war about such things as the Sunday closing of saloons, the existence of gambling and commercialized vice and the distribution of political patronage, the town's educational needs were completely ignored. Teachers were underpaid and therefore inefficient, and school principals changed continuously because the post was a political plum.

Ultimately, and largely because Harlan urged it and worked for it, Verity accepted membership on the town's school board.

Meantime, however, he proceeded with his own ideas as to how to help improve the community. What he had in mind was the encouragement of some sort of mutual-interest organization among his own employees which would enable them to enrich their lives outside the plant.

"You can't force improvement on people, no matter how necessary or desirable it may be," he said. "They'll resent it if you try it."

Then once more there was a parade in Middletown—and it provided him with the opportunity he was seeking.

This parade—on July 4, 1903—was a celebration of Middletown's centenary, a festival in which prizes were offered for the best floats and the largest groups in the parade. The Armco employees won twenty dollars and were so jubilant that they sent a delegation to Verity's home to notify him of this success. He offered to add eighty dollars to the sum as a nest egg for the launching of an employees' club. About a week later, some eighty employees met in a lodge hall and formed what they called the "American Rolling Mill Mutual Benefit Association of Middletown, Ohio," a big mouthful for a club with a one-hundred-dollar treasury.

Within a year there were two hundred members in the "Armco Association," as it was later called. Though organized originally as a mutual-benefit insurance association, it rapidly became a social and recreational organization, retaining, however, all of its original features.

When the members staged their first party and introduced their families to the boss, he told them:

"There is nothing one can do for himself, in this world, that begins to give the pleasure and satisfaction that one little unselfish effort 'for some other fellow' will bring.

"I'm sure every one of you has tried it. If not, try it without delay; you cannot afford to miss the sensation.

"It takes many men of many minds and all sorts of hearts to make up a business world, but of all others give me the man who treats his fellow men with honesty, courtesy and consideration, and I'll take chances on all his other characteristics."

Shortly after he made this speech, he learned that, not only is the business world made up of many men of many minds, but that many of the minds function strangely. For, in no time at all, some employers in the area were damning him and his theories as "visionary" and "crack-brained" and even "socialistic."

He had to defend himself even in his own company. His defense was that an employer's demonstration of fairness, frankness, and willingness to understand employees' problems was the soundest investment he knew how to make. Eventually he convinced the opposition and was able to inform the board of governors of the Association that the company would match the members' dues, dollar for dollar. This was done because of his conviction that it was an employer's duty to help employees help themselves in times of sickness and bereavement. This was done at least a decade before the states began enactment of Workmen's Compensation Laws.

As this employee-directed Association grew, its social base was broadened. It sponsored sports programs, parties, study clubs, drama and music festivals, and the thousand and one extra-curricular projects in which men and women engage in the pursuit of happiness. In all these activities there was always the unobtrusive hand of George Verity, doing a bit here and a bit there but never doing so much at one time that the beneficiaries might resent his help as interference or paternalism.

"People," he said, "are happiest when they feel they are creating their own happiness."

When he said such things in the early years, young Charlie Hook seemed to understand him best and to agree with him most strongly.

It was Hook's understanding of and belief in the Verity theories that led to the company's pioneering in the first application of that now widely accepted practice called "employee representation." The success of this first practical industrial democracy stemmed from the fact that the men themselves made it work.

It started because John Hogan's engine was too feeble for the extra tasks sometimes imposed on it. If the crews of two mills thrust bars into mills simultaneously, the underpowered engine would snort, gasp and stop, usually on dead center. Whenever that happened, all production stopped while men worked hard and long to disengage the metal and start the engine again. Not infrequently it damaged machinery seriously.

In time, men learned to co-operate by watching one another and maintaining a proper sequence of operations. Unfortunately, however, the staff always included a number of rugged individualists who made, and lived according to, their own rules. To curb them, Hook posted a notice that any man responsible for stalling the engine would be suspended from three to thirty days, according to the individual's carelessness.

Almost invariably, after a man was suspended, someone would come to Hook and tell him that the wrong man had been punished.

"I'm sorry," he would reply, "but it isn't my fault. I shouldn't be astonished to learn that I'm punishing the wrong man at least eighty per cent of the time; but I can't hope to be just unless I'm told who the culprits are."

"We don't like to squeal on a guy," they would reply. And

to that he countered with the observation that he respected them for it.

Ultimately Charlie Hook worked out a plan and presented it to them for their consideration. When his suggested plan was presented to them, he made it clear that its success would depend on the manner in which they handled it.

"We all know what this stalling of the engine is costing you in lost tonnage," he said. "You are in better position to identify the non-cooperators than I am; so I am proposing that you appoint a committee of three to serve on each turn and that these committees determine who is at fault when the engine stops and what the penalty shall be. The management will always back up the decisions of your committees."

Thereafter there were more men suspended and for longer periods than when Hook had been handling the problem himself. The plan of democratic self-discipline worked so well that the trouble was virtually eliminated in a few months.

One morning shortly after the plan went into effect, Hook, coming to work, met Billy Stringham, the veteran roller, going home. Stringham, who later became a company official, should have been going to work, for he was not only working on the day turn, but was chairman of the committee of engine-coddling on that turn.

"What's the matter, Billy?" Hook asked. "Are you sick?"

With blistering adjectives that expressed his disgust inadequately, Billy announced he was indeed sick because he had stalled the engine—and laid himself off for three days.

Thus introduced, the idea grew naturally into an "Advisory

Committee Plan." Later, when Hook became assistant general superintendent, and there were five hundred employees, it was apparent that, for some reason, the gulf between management and men was again widening.

One day he sauntered out into the sheet-mill department where he had begun his Armco service and asked some of the Amalgamated officials if it would be possible for them to grant him the privilege of attending the union lodge meeting that night.

The suggestion almost bowled them over. They had never heard of such a thing as a representative of a company's management attending a union meeting, they said.

"My God, Charlie!" they said. "It just ain't done!"

"Suppose we break precedent and make a start," he said. "We're getting too busy around here to stop and talk to each other about our troubles as we used to do. I'd like to hear about your problems, and I believe you're still interested in mine. Can't we get together in that way?"

They scratched their heads. They wondered out loud if their union's national laws permitted such an unheard-of thing. They said they'd have to take up such a weighty issue at a special meeting.

"What does your union stand for?" he asked. "Isn't it a constructive organization designed for our mutual interest? Surely it isn't merely a grievance committee designed to squeeze all the wages it can out of an employer!"

Upshot of all this was that he was invited to attend and called on to speak. Given the privilege of the floor, he suggested that the lodge elect an advisory committee to meet him once a week. When that committee reported he asked them if they had any suggestions as to how their department's operations could be improved.

They tumbled out more suggestions than he could handle, and, as other meetings followed, improvements were made, confidence replaced suspicion and matters of much importance were discussed.

Before long, each department had its advisory committee for which members were elected by secret ballot for a year of service. This democratic method, which was improved and refined in later years, was the source of great consternation among men who met it for the first time.

A. K. Lewis, later an official of the company, came to the mill as a draughtsman via apprenticeship in mills in Birmingham and Pueblo, and was almost floored with amazement to see a steel company doing things democratically instead of dictatorially. In mills where he had worked, owners never came near the place. Here, everyone had access to both the Verity and Hook offices, and there seemed to be no clear-cut distinction between management and men.

"It seemed to me," he said, "that a lot of time was being wasted here in committees; and it took me a long time to realize how really ignorant I had been of sound principles of management before I came here."

Tommy Grubbs was a roving sheet-heater who "thought the only people who ever stuck to one mill were the majority stockholders." A union man who had lost two jobs in strikes and had once been badly beaten on a picket line, he came to Middletown on an excursion trip to look this mill over when a trust snapped up the Pennsylvania mill in which he was working.

Reporting to his buddies in the East, Tommy said: "You won't believe this, but it's true. The men in this mill actually like to teach one another the tricks of their trade! It's the damnedest place you ever saw!"

In all, almost sixty of Tommy's buddies chucked their jobs and came out to see for themselves. Not a few of them remained for many years.

When Strawbridge left finally in 1904 to start a mill of his own in Maryland, several men went with him. But, one by one, they came back to this place where, as Albert A. Meahl, the pair-heater, put it:

"The wages weren't so high and the prospects didn't look so good, but a man was treated like a human being instead of a stock pile or a machine, and the president wasn't too important to stop his buggy and give a guy a lift when he saw him walking to work."

8

Figures and Frontiers

No, the prospects were none too promising in the early years. Better than figures of speech, the speech of figures describes them.

Consider the figures:

Of steel—all kinds—the nation's mills were capable of making eleven million tons in 1901. In the previous year, Carnegie's forges alone spewed out three million tons. And here was this little one-horse mill, trying to produce nine hundred tons a month—and taking nine months to produce what Carnegie had been producing in twenty-four hours before he sold out to an even larger outfit.

Even through the rose-colored glasses of hope it was plain that the Verity "board of strategy" had to scrabble fast for a sure-fire formula for survival, or else——!

Quantity production was obviously not their business. So, by force of circumstance, they had to think of themselves as quality specialists. In that way, they pioneered perforce on frontiers of steel research.

In one of those early committee meetings, someone observed that a gate to such a frontier was open—perhaps not wide enough for a big steel producer to get through, but certainly wide enough for a small and agile outfit to creep in.

"The electrical industry," said this forgotten someone, "seems to be having difficulty getting sheet steel for dynamos, motors, generators and transformers. It doesn't use a lot of steel, and is pretty particular about what electrical engineers call 'definite and controlled magnetic permeability' in the steel it buys, so the big tonnage producers are saying to hell with it."

Hearing which, George Verity and Bob Carnahan put their heads together and studied the steel needs of those strange newcomers in the industrial ranks, the power providers.

They learned that the electrical industry was indeed an insignificant consumer of sheet steel, and apparently doomed to remain small and insignificant because sheets made from Bessemer steel had such poor magnetic quality that they functioned faultily at best when used as the laminated hearts of power machines then coming into use.

But what was this magnetic permeability that the power providers deemed so important a quality of steel? Why was it so essential? And what did one do to steel to give it this quality?

Questions such as these flew thick and fast across the table in George Verity's office where the strategists talked far into the night. But there were no answers to any of the questions, for this was 1902, and, though electric lights and telephones and trolley cars were becoming fairly common things, the force that made them work was still largely magic to the people who used the devices. It was a force suspect by laymen. People still talked of "the fool experiments" of Edison, took the receivers off their hooks and let them dangle in a thunderstorm, and nursed the fear that electricity leaked subtly and dangerously into the house if the switch was turned on while there was no bulb in the socket.

Though the Verity strategists' electrical lore was not quite on that low level, it was too weak to enable them to get their teeth into this tough problem.

So, in the fall of that year, they selected salesman Phillips as the man to visit George Westinghouse's famous group of electrical experimenters and try to find out what kind of steel was needed and what one had to do to iron to give it proper magnetic permeability.

There was not enough money in the treasury to permit Phillips to ride in a Pullman, so he went in a day coach, taking along the company's offer to undertake experimental production of steel sheets with controlled electrical quality.

Amazement is a weak word for the Westinghouse reaction to the offer. Since 1900, electrical pioneers had despaired of ever getting the kind of steel they needed from American steelmakers and were pretty much resigned to the prospect of having to buy it in Europe at high prices topped with tariff duties.

To salesman Phillips, Westinghouse engineer Wesley J. Beck explained what was needed and why.

The electrical industry's need arose from the fact that man's employment of this invisible energy was then expanding into new fields.

When George Verity was born, men were using the force mainly for communication. In that year, when telegrapher Edison converted Morse dots and dashes into the news of Lincoln's assassination, George Westinghouse left a Navy Department clerkship, returned to his father's home and, reading a magazine article's description of the use of compressed air in the digging of an Alpine tunnel, began to dream of what crusty old Commodore Cornelius Vanderbilt later called "the damned fool idea of stopping trains with wind."

By the time George Verity had taken charge of the Standish store, Edison had harnessed the force for illumination, Alexander Graham Bell had expanded its use in communication, and men like Leo Daft, Frank Julian Sprague, Stephen Field and others had put it to work in transportation.

The pioneering of these men then brought up three major uncertainties about electricity—uncertainties expressed in the questions:

What will be its chief use?

In what form should it be generated?

How shall it be transmitted efficiently?

Out of these questions grew a bitter quarrel over the relative merits of direct and alternating current—a quarrel without meaning to plain people who wondered why Edison and Lord Kelvin clashed so heatedly with Elihu Thomson and Nikola Tesla and Westinghouse.

That plain people heard of the quarrel at all was due only to its involvement of the then already famous names, Edison and Westinghouse—Edison, "the electrical wizard," and Westinghouse, "the man who made railway travel safe." But the reasons for the quarrel were mainly beyond their ken.

Direct current had been favored originally because it was the only known form of energy in the early days of electrical development. Early dynamos generated it, principally because earlier batteries had produced it. So, early motors were built to use it. There seemed to be no way of breaking away from custom until Thomson built a three-coil dynamo that led to development of the single-phase induction motor, and Tesla, the Serbian inventor, interested Westinghouse in his "ridiculous" brushless motor.

Thereafter, though Edison continued to get the plaudits of laymen, Westinghouse solved the problem of power transmission—solved it because he had an uncanny ability to bring proudly individualistic inventors together and make them cooperate by pooling creative abilities in organized industrial research.

The solution of the problem was difficult. Electric energy was expensive to produce and the loss was cumulatively great according to the length of wire used to transmit it. To get the solution, the Westinghouse "geniuses" reached all the way back to an amusing laboratory trick called "electromagnetic induction" which Michael Faraday discovered as long ago as the year in which Grandfather Matthew Verity moved to America.

In Europe Westinghouse saw a crude machine called a "secondary generator," which, employing Faraday's discovery, was brought to the Pittsburgh laboratories and developed into the modern transformer. With this device, having nothing to do with energy production, electrical impulses could be transformed to high voltage for efficient, long-range transmission and again transformed to low voltage at the point of use. Installed first in an experimental line at Great Barrington, Vermont, in 1885, the transformer, linked ten years later to other devices nurtured by the Westinghouse engineers, resulted in the harnessing of Niagara's tremendous power.

Now, here was this enormous potential of power, waiting to serve mankind but shackled because no steel was available for the specific needs of machines which depended on fine control of magnetism for their efficiency.

The magnetic properties of iron had been known for decades. Early dynamos used solid iron forgings as permanent magnets but their ponderous weight was accompanied by weak power because the heat of magnetic friction debilitated their strength progressively. To reduce this power-stealing heat, laminated sheets of iron were tried. The results were so encouraging that solid forgings were at last abandoned, bringing up the problem awaiting solution in 1902.

Most steel sheets then manufactured were products of Bessemer converters. They were useless because almost no two sheets had the same magnetic qualities. The advent of the open-hearth process stirred the hopes of Westinghouse engineers but the quantity producers of steel blasted the hopes, even after they began to install open-hearth furnaces.

In view of the steel industry's great expansion in those years, the attitude of the tonnage producers was reasonable. By comparison with most steel-consuming industries, the infant electrical industry was a peanut stand. Moreover, its demands were exacting. It wanted wafer-thin sheets. It asked for steel with less than .08 per cent carbon, a manganese content between .35 and .50 per cent, and little sulphur or phosphorus. To make such steel, only clean scrap and carefully prepared pig iron could be used, all melting and heating processes had to be controlled to curtail carbon content and all fuels had to be checked for traces of sulphur.

All these quibbles about a few dribbles of steel? To hell with it! said steelmakers.

That was the problem as the Westinghouse engineers explained it to Phillips.

At the Westinghouse works it was chubby, good-natured Wesley Beck's peculiar problem. This young Hoosier had come to Westinghouse from Purdue University to take up five years of apprentice training. It was considered high privilege to be allowed to work with the Westinghouse wizards. Beginners were paid five cents an hour while enjoying the privilege. If they showed promise at the end of three months, their pay was raised—to eight cents an hour. It was a tough school. In it, George Westinghouse winnowed out the ordinary humans who work for mere money and caught those extraordinary humans who work for the fun of it.

Under the severe discipline of the plan, Beck worked hard and was finally rewarded in 1899 with a job in the engineering department. His reward was the dubious one of shouldering responsibility for the magnetic property of all steel purchases. The job threw him into daily contact with Pittsburgh steelmakers and, though he learned much about steelmaking processes, he found those worthies so blind to his vision of what the future of electricity might be that he despaired of ever encountering one of the breed with enough intelligence or interest to try to understand his company's needs.

Great, therefore, was his amazement when the usually impeccable Phillips, rumpled by a sleeper-jump in a day coach, tumbled out samples of Armco's open-hearth steel for analysis and added George Verity's offer to co-operate in any experiments that Westinghouse might want to undertake.

The suggestion of co-operative research was language that Westinghouse men understood. When they recovered from their astonishment, they ordered Beck to pack his duffel and move to Middletown to supervise manufacture of test sheets from scrap pile to finished product.

One April day in 1903 he was introduced to Carnahan. Bob moved an extra cot into his office and, tossing Beck's luggage under it, said:

"This is where I live. Make yourself at home. Let's get to work."

The Carnahan gesture pleased Beck immensely. After an introduction to George Verity and an inspection tour of the plant, he turned to Carnahan and said:

"I think I'm going to like this place. It's not a steel mill. It's a life-size research laboratory in the rough."

Of this laboratory in the rough, Bob Carnahan was the chief

of research. His chief assistant was a man whose entire academic education did not exceed six months of the rudimentary lore haphazardly offered in a one-room rural school in Indiana.

This man was Orley Harvey Moles, who came to George Verity on September 10, 1900, and dug ditches and poured concrete while awaiting the day when he could handle the ladle for the first heat.

Born on a farm in Franklin County, Indiana, in September, 1870, he was taken to Decatur, Alabama, in 1878, by his father who had the crazy notion—fairly common in the tragic era of reconstruction—that the beaten South would provide great opportunity for an ambitious Northern farmer. The opportunity turned out to be a chance to share the South's grinding poverty. It killed Orley's father, then his mother, and the four orphaned children were taken in by a plantation owner who put them all to work in the cotton fields.

From this slavery Orley ran away at sixteen and worked in a cotton gin until the plantation owner caught up with him and seized his wage of ten dollars a month. He ran away again and wandered north. Into Missouri, where he worked briefly clearing land, and across Illinois he roved until he reached a farm in southern Indiana, where he was again virtually enslaved. Once more he ran away, landed in Muncie, penniless, and found a job in a steel mill. That was in 1892, and thenceforth molten steel's "lovely smell"—as he called it—was never far from his nose.

After six years of learning what he could pick up, he was able to get a better job at Carnegie's Homestead Works, where a heat leaped out of control and burned the heel off one of his feet. After months in a hospital, he came out to find his world of steel in a boiling mess of mergers. So he drifted from mill to mill, improving his knowledge and seeking an employer who would appreciate his skills. In South Chicago he met a melter who had helped him when he was a boy in the Muncie mill.

"There's a new mill starting in Middletown," said the melter. "They need a first ladleman, I hear."

Orley came, met George Verity and decided this was the employer he had been seeking all along. Then he met Carnahan, and the two men, so dissimilar in training and background, were instantly drawn toward each other in a bond of affection which had become brotherly by the time the experimental furnace was built.

"I'm going to make a furnaceman out of you," said Carnahan after Orley handled the ladle on that night when the first heat was tapped. Between turns he taught him "the tricks" and then put him on as second helper.

On the night when the first helper burned the roof out of the furnace, Carnahan exploded, threw the man out, and, turning to Orley, said:

"Now you're the first helper."

"Please, Mr. Carnahan," Orley replied, "I can't handle it. I couldn't bear to hurt a furnace."

The plea pulled Carnahan up short. Here, he realized, was a man whose love for that brain child of his was as deep and as fierce as his own. Putting his arm around Orley's shoulder, he said:

"I swear I'll curb my temper even if you burn her to the ground."

On May 9, 1903, after Beck and Carnahan had worked a month on the preliminary preparations for a test heat of electrical steel, Carnahan came down from his office bedroom in the small hours and found Orley doing the melter's work in addition to his own.

"Where's the melter?" he demanded.

"I don't know," said Orley.

"I think you're lying to protect him," said Bob, launching himself into a torrent of maledictions, including a few blistering descriptions of Orley's ancestry. Then the irascible man stormed through the mill, found the melter snoring on a pile of bricks, and, hustling the bewildered aristocrat of steel through the mill, heaved him into the street.

Returning to Orley, he said:

"I apologize for what I said. From now on, you're a melter."

A few nights later, all was in readiness for the great experiment. The raw materials—ore, scrap, pig iron and fuel—had been chosen as carefully as the ingredients of a doctor's prescription. The first batch of iron brew, confected especially for the electrical industry, was bubbling in the furnace. His nerves raw with tension, Carnahan proposed a buggy ride in the country. Beck accepted the invitation gladly.

Near midnight the two of them returned by way of the open-hearth department. There the reassuringly dependable Orley peered into the man-made Gehenna and said the brew would be ready in a few hours—if the furnace didn't melt into it.

"I'll call you," he said, and Beck and Carnahan retired.

Beck's slumber was torn asunder by the clangor of a bell and Carnahan's roar. The noise actually dumped him out of bed. It was one o'clock. He started to dress.

"Don't dress, dammit!" Carnahan shouted, leaping for the door. "Pull your britches over your nightshirt and get downstairs in a hurry. We might lose the heat!"

Occasion for Carnahan's alarm was the unprecedentedly high temperature to which this brew had to be brought to burn out the so-called impurities, for refractory materials were not then very efficient, and superheated metal had a nasty habit of burning its way out into places where it caused great damage and endangered lives. Even when furnaces withstood its attack, it sometimes bored right through the bottoms of ladles when tapped.

The furnace and ladle held it that night, but the problems of George Verity and his daring experimenters were far from done. Indeed, they had only begun; for, to make this magnetic steel, silicon was used to burn out the impurities, and this silicon not only increased temperatures dangerously but produced a steel which exploded into gravel when moisture touched its hot surface.

The introduction of silicon to improve iron's magnetic quality was the result of clews dug up from several sources by the strategists who gathered regularly in the Verity office to compare notes and propose fantastic ideas. Tracing these clews, they found a curiously interlocked pattern of developments which, though apparently unrelated, were actually tightly interwoven causes and effects.

Here, as briefly as possible and with minimum concern for technical detail, are the outlines of the findings.

In 1861 Sir Henry Bessemer observed that silicon prevented blowholes in castings, but it meant little because silicon was rare. In 1882 Sir Robert Hadfield, puzzled by the way in which a pair of steel rolling-mill pinions eroded their housings, analyzed their steel, discovered a content of 1.5 per cent silicon and began dreaming of producing superior grinding wheels by increasing iron's silicon content.

But Sir Robert had to drop the idea because silicon was a laboratory curiosity sold at $100 an ounce. About the time he turned away from this idea to pursue the researches that led to his important development of manganese steel, Westinghouse was tapping Niagara for power. This opened up a new field for electricity—the production of great heat. Lured to Niagara by this heat potential, Alfred and Eugene Cowles, who had been working with Charles Hall on the Oberlin College attempts to produce aluminum electrically, set up an electric furnace and produced an abrasive which they incorrectly called "crystallized silicon."

Here was the stuff for those superior grinding wheels that Sir Robert had hoped to produce by combining iron and silicon, but it was not "crystallized silicon." Nor was it "diamond dust" as A. E. Acheson believed it to be when, shortly afterward, he found it sticking to a carbon rod with which he had given a lump of clay an electric shock. Though diamond polishers bought

Acheson's first batch of the mysterious stuff by the carat at $560 a pound, he soon had commercial furnaces going at Niagara and was turning it out in ten-ton batches at ten cents a pound. It was silicon carbide, a better abrasive than man had known before.

The Westinghouse transmission lines and transformers had made this possible. Now comes the most amazing sequence of events; for, over there in Pittsburgh were the Westinghouse scientists seeking better steel for transformers, and, up here at Niagara, electric furnaces were building up higher temperatures than man had ever handled before—building them up to make better abrasives—*and accidentally producing pure silicon.*

Exactly at the moment when the Verity strategists were hitting on the need for this rare stuff to make electrical steel, the electric furnaces at Niagara were turning it out in such large batches that its price fell from $100 an ounce to $0.10 a pound. And, before long, ferrosilicon, an alloy of iron and silicon, was freely used as a deoxidizing agent in the manufacture of steel.

The Armco experimenters found that, though the ferrosilicon improved steel's magnetic permeability, it could not be added to the brew in the furnace without destroying furnace linings. Tossed into ladles after tapping, it shot temperature up to a point where ladle linings collapsed. Added to the steel in the molds, it had to be handled with great care to result in uniform structure of the ingots.

(Another link in the peculiar sequence of events is the fact that Niagara's electric furnaces subsequently produced the very refractory materials required to enable open-hearth furnaces and ladles to handle electrical steels subjected to the high temperatures induced by ferrosilicon. But that came later.)

On top of their troubles with high temperatures, the Verity strategists had their hands full of other problems. Their high-silicon steel was brittle and coarse-grained. It shattered like glass when water touched it, so it had to be air-cooled. Much time was thus lost and much valuable equipment had to stand idle for long periods. Handled hot, ingots often cracked in the soaking furnaces. They had to be rolled so hot on the bar mills that they often snaked into collars, wrecking rolls and mills, to say nothing of rollers' dispositions. Rolls and plates of conveyor tables buckled and warped frightfully under the hot bars.

To get an idea of the hazards involved, imagine men handling 200-pound ingots and bars, mainly by muscular force, and handling them so hot that molten steel sometimes dripped off the surfaces.

Before delivery to sheet mills, the bars were again air-cooled, and once more sorely needed equipment stood idle as bars cooled to blackness and then gathered thin films of red rust. "Red devils" the men called them.

They were so full of devilish tricks that they raised continuous hell with orderly processes. They wrecked equipment, and time and again they almost wrecked the fragile tissue of human loyalties which George Verity was trying to weave into the company's chain-mail armor. He was much among the men in these trying times. And the men, keenly aware of the fact that they were participating in a life-and-death struggle with an experiment that *had* to succeed, stuck to their jobs with the grim determination of men resigned to the prospect of going down with the ship.

The fidelity of the men hinged on little things, such as an incident in the remembered yesterdays of George Krebs.

George, who was a pair-heater then, had come to the end of one trying day in the full heat of midsummer when bearded old Dan Fisher, the foreman who had been an English roller, came to him and said the mill was going to be shorthanded on the next turn because many of the night crew were sick.

"I wish you'd stay and help us out," said Dan. "I know you're dog-tired, and I hate to ask you, but I need you badly."

In all, George and five others stayed another twelve hours, wrestling with the red devils until they were reeling with weariness. When the night was done, Dan came up to them, shook their hands and said:

"This will not be forgotten, boys."

A few weeks later the six had forgotten it. Summoned to report to Hook's office, they went in, wondering why they were being called on the carpet. Then Charlie Hook came in, shook their hands and presented each of them with a silver cup engraved with the company's thanks for what they had done.

Every morning and every evening George Verity stood at the gate and greeted all of them, giving them the opportunity to air their grievances.

Once Billy DuChemin was standing beside him when one of Billy's men passed and shot him an ugly look. Verity saw it and asked Billy what it meant.

"I can't understand that man," said Billy. "He's a good workman but there are times when he's downright mean in his demands for trouble. I don't know how to handle him."

"Billy," said Verity, "that man has been mistreated. You must try to understand him even if it's difficult. If he can't stand fair treatment we'll have to replace him with someone who can. But I don't believe that's necessary. I don't believe there's a man on earth who can hold out against kindness."

The quiet sincerity with which it was said bothered Billy—bothered him so much that he invited the man into his office and blurted it out.

There was a long silence in which the man stared hard at the floor and twisted his cap in his hands. Then, looking up, he said, "Bill, I'm sorry!" And the two of them shook hands and were good friends for years after.

Ultimately, the red devils were mastered. Because they were, the efficiency of electrical machinery improved 50 per cent in the next two years. Now the invisible horses, which Michael Faraday had first glimpsed in their roles as servants of mankind, could leap forward to the multitudinous tasks waiting for them in millions of motors, generators, transformers and countless useful appliances that serve common people in so many ways nowadays.

It was no small achievement. Without it, a one-half-horsepower motor could not have been reduced to the diminutive thing that powers the housewife's washing machine. Nor could the transformers of 1900 have been refined into the tiny watch-like things now performing in radio sets. It has been estimated that if electrical illumination alone received by Americans in 1939 had been furnished by the power equipment of 1900, the additional cost would have exceeded fifteen billion dollars.

It was well for George Verity's company that the experiment succeeded when it did. It had taken about three years for his associates to "iron the bugs out of their mechanical processes," and for him to win the confidence of the men. In those three years there had been a perpetual shortage of working capital.

At the end of the third year the sheet-rolling capacity had improved to such a degree that the melting facilities had to be expanded. Carnahan enlarged the original furnace to handle fifty tons. It was not large enough, and two more were built. Then they found themselves able to make more steel than they could roll, and they looked around for a mill that needed bars. The mill they found was at Zanesville. Occupying one of the sites which had been originally offered to Verity, it had ample rolling mills but lacked furnaces. It was just what they needed, and they were just what the mill at Zanesville needed.

Just as the Verity associates were congratulating themselves about the lucky find, adversity hit them again.

On July 30, 1904, when they felt they were at last winning the long fight with the red devils, a fire broke out and threatened to destroy the whole works. Engineer John Hogan ran from his home when he heard the alarm and didn't stop running until he had darted into the inferno and shut down the engine whose running was spreading the fire and endangering lives.

They dragged him out more dead than alive, and he smiled and thanked his rescuers with a bit of blarney, though he was horribly burned and in great pain.

Then, while they were down, they were kicked by a collapse of the market for sheet bars. It came about because the big steelmakers had come around finally to the use of the basic open-hearth process in which the Verity outfit had pioneered. In this their extremity, they were drawn still closer to co-operation with W. S. Horner and his associates in the Zanesville mill, where there was a need for the sheet bars of which Armco had a surplus. Early in 1905 a merger was proposed. In June it was consummated.

William Simpson agreed to go to Zanesville and take charge of this plant which eventually became the center of the company's electrical steel manufacture and research.

The merger involved merely an exchange of securities. Additional stock was issued and enough new working capital was provided to enable the company to pay off its accumulated indebtedness. The company's capacity was now 3,300 tons a month. Capitalization had expanded from $500,000 to $1,400,000. Employment had increased from 350 to 1,000. Pay rolls, which had been $196,271 in 1901, were $409,278 in 1905. There were now two plants, complementing each other.

The first five years were history. Looking back at them, George Verity again had the strange sensation of having read about these things as happening to some fictional character. Just when prospects looked blackest in 1904 this windfall of a merger had come, doubling capacity with no increase of overhead.

Well-wishers praised him for good planning.

"Planning?" he said, laughing. "I did no planning. These things just happened so."

It had been a period of pioneering. Technically, the pioneering began with the daring use of the open-hearth furnace and the linking of that process with others in a continuous chain of operations. Socially, the pioneering expressed itself in unusually humane relations between management and men. Once a year the men met with the management and all cards were laid on the table for discussion and adjustment of wages. Each year there was a slight improvement, even though the period had been one of penury.

The first six months were recorded in red ink—a loss of $75,000. Red became black at the first year's end when the books showed a profit of $150,000. The profit was paper merely, as was the profit of every quarter thereafter in the first five years; for, as fast as earnings piled up, they were plowed back into the business—into equipment, supplies, better wages.

During the first five years of grueling work, Major Lloyd had wearied of this profitless business and expressed a wish to retire. Verity and Simpson took up an option which the Major gave them on his stock and this enabled each of them to bring his holdings up to 500 shares. A joint loan was effected to take care of this purchase.

During the first five years, Verity's salary had never exceeded $3,600 a year. It did not begin to cover the obligations that quickly piled up in his new responsibilities. At the beginning of this second five-year period, with the business so greatly enlarged and strengthened through the Zanesville merger, the company's board of directors felt his salary should now be more commensurate with his responsibilities.

9

A Job for John

TO THE eyes of the young—and of the young in heart—the fiery birth of steel is a sight endlessly fascinating.

For adventurous youth of Middletown and environs this Curtis Street plant—the first steel mill in this part of America—was a magnet from the start. Toward the end of the first five-year period, when news of fabulous feats performed here in electrical sheet experiments had begun to spread far and wide, the pull was irresistible. More and more young men came to the plant—some to watch and worship the heroic men who participated in steel's infernal birth, and some to seek work.

At first there was no fence around the property, and sightseers often wandered into dangerous places, especially in the open-hearth department at the north end of the building.

One morning a dapper young man, attired in what was then called an "ice-cream suit," strode through the mill as if he were an owner inspecting his property.

"Who's the dude?" said the men, staring.

Into the open-hearth department he strutted, imperiously deaf to the same question shouted by the melter and his helpers.

Suddenly the shouts died. The men gasped. The visitor had vanished before their eyes—vanished as if the earth had opened up and swallowed him.

Actually, it had. When the men ran out to look for him, they found he had walked out on a weak spot in the buried brickwork of the large tunnel that fed the furnaces, and that it had caved in under his weight. They fished him out quickly. Though he looked like a chimney sweep, he was apparently unhurt, for he fairly flew away from there and was never seen or heard of again.

After that amusing but rather dangerous incident, a fence was built around the entire property and visitors were provided with passes and guides.

Early in June of 1904, a tall, handsome young man called on Verity and asked for a job. Knowing the young man and the environment from which he came, the president was astonished by the request. Assuming that the job seeker wanted a place in the office, Verity explained that there was no vacancy at the time in the office staff and that there was little likelihood that one would soon develop in the rather small clerical force.

To this, the young man's amazing rejoinder was that he was not seeking a soft, swivel-chair post but a chance to work in the mill.

"If that is what you want," said Verity, "see Charlie Hook, the superintendent of the sheet mills. He can tell you if there's an opening for you."

"Thank you!" exclaimed the young man. The ring of undisguised joy in the exclamation added to the president's puzzlement.

This young man was John Butler Tytus. He was born in

Middietown on December 6, 1875. The son of a locally prominent family, he possessed a Yale Bachelor of Arts degree, and was apparently destined to follow his ancestral profession—the manufacture of paper.

Had Verity asked him why he sought hard and heavy work in the sheet mills, he could not have explained, he admitted later. For there was a restlessness in him that defied explanation. He was twenty-nine and dissatisfied with himself. After Yale, he had worked five years in his father's paper mill. It was work which somehow could not hold his interest. Then for two years he had worked for a general contractor in the construction field. This, too, palled.

Somehow the siren song of hot mill rolls biting into glowing bars of steel reached his ears. Several times he visited the Armco plant and watched, fascinated, as hot mill crews patiently and laboriously passed bars of red-hot steel back and forth. Seeing the incandescent bars become thinner and longer under the squeeze of the wringerlike rolls, he wondered why steel sheets had to be rolled in that time-honored but time-wasting way.

Was there a better way? In the back of his mind the question linked itself into his knowledge of the way in which a porridge of water-soaked wood pulp becomes a continuous sheet of paper on the great Fourdriniers in the paper mills.

"When I first visited the steel mill," he said later, "I counted sheets being handled twenty-two different times. Right then and there I figured that a business which had so much lost motion had plenty of future for a young man."

Because he was ignorant of the reasons for the sheet-rolling methods, he added, he was positive that they could be easily improved.

"But I learned!" he said. "And as I learned, I became less cocksure."

After leaving Verity, Tytus visited Hook's office. Hook knew who he was but had at that time no personal acquaintance with him.

It was now Charlie's turn to be amazed by John's request, for the man who was asking for a job as a beginner was the superintendent's senior by five years. Trying to discourage the applicant, Hook described fully the character of the work on the sheet mills and added that it would be a long and difficult task for a man of John's age and education to adapt himself to the hard and heavy work.

Tytus listened attentively and replied that in spite of the enumerated difficulties he would like an opportunity to see what he could do.

"It's a tough game!" Hook warned.

"Undoubtedly," John replied.

"It will break your back!"

"Perhaps. But I want to try it."

One morning soon afterward, it was the bulge-muscled rollers' turn to register amazement when the slim, handsome Tytus, wearing new canvas gloves on his soft, white hands, was introduced to them as a "spare hand." (A spare hand was a novice helper who took the place of any member of a sheet-mill crew who might be absent. Such jobs did not provide fulltime employment.)

To this thoroughbred, pastured among Percherons, the usual horseplay of steel-mill initiation was of course applied with gusto. But he soon acquired a reputation for being good-naturedly disinterested in nonsense.

Though the men did not understand him, they learned to respect him, for he never shirked and his hands were soon as leathery as the best of them. He applied himself so earnestly that he was put on a regular turn as a doubler, one of the hardest tasks on the old manual mills. Promoted regularly thereafter, he worked on enough different jobs to have acquired a solid foundation of sheet-mill practice by the end of eighteen months.

In those eighteen months, John Tytus learned the reasons for methods which he had deemed somewhat ridiculous. He had learned by participating in every last one of the operations—pounding knowledge into his brain by feeling facts with blistered fingers and telegraphing them to his weary mind through aching muscles.

Studying all aspects of his various jobs, he asked many questions, some of them ridiculous to mill men. So, in time, he learned much of the history of rolling steel sheets.

Originally, flat sheets had been made by hammering hot iron bars until they were thin enough. This method had declined when some forgotten genius hit upon the idea of squeezing hot iron between rolls. For many years after that discovery, about the only change in rolling had been the transition from water to steam as power for turning the rolls. Sizes, weights, durability of rolls, housings and couplings had increased, and the output had been improved thereby, but the old methods, established by the clannish Welsh rollers, remained unchanged.

As they had been for decades, red-hot bars, held by hand with long-handled tongs, were passed back and forth through large rolls. Giant screws in the housings that held the rolls were turned down between passes to "increase draft" (diminish space between rolls) until the resultant plate or heavy sheet was thinned as far as possible. Reheated, the sheets were doubled, or folded back upon themselves into a "pack," and rolled back and forth again. The thinner the sheets had to be, the more the several operations had to be repeated. Since all of the operations called for exceptional skill, great strength and endurance, sheet-mill operators were well-paid aristocrats of the world of steel and sheets were costly products.

After sheet-mill crews were through with their part of the operations and the openers had separated the folded packs, the shearmen lopped off ragged edges and squared the sheets to required sizes. Then the annealers and picklers and galvanizers had to perform their tasks. Before an article made of galvanized or black sheet steel reached the ultimate consumer, much human effort had been put into it.

Charlie Hook became deeply interested in John's progress in the mill, watching both his work and his attitude toward his associates. Hook realized that if a man of John's education and ability had it in him to master the difficult techniques of sheet-mill practice, he might easily prove to be of great value to the company.

By December, 1905, Tytus had gained enough experience and had so thoroughly proved his adaptability to exacting demands that Hook made him his first assistant.

Thus thrown closer together, the two men became better acquainted and acquired more opportunities for exchange of ideas. Tytus possessed one trait which Hook deemed significant. John's imaginative powers were unbounded. He was a persistent experimenter—so much so that Hook found it difficult at times to keep him well within practical limits. But, in the main, he encouraged John in every way he could.

"He was always searching for better ways of doing things," Hook recalls.

In time, the two men came to share their dreams and hopes, talking things over in Hook's stuffy, greasy little office alongside the clattering hot mills. There, one night, after they had let their imaginations rove far and wide, John said:

"Some day, Charlie, we'll be making sheets in long strips like they make paper."

The remark struck a responsive chord. As a young man, Hook had been able to get into a mill where an attempt had been made to roll sheets continuously, that is, by placing one stand of mills in front of another, instead of passing bars and sheets back and forth through one single stand of mills. There had been several such experiments throughout the world of steel, and, though all had been expensive and all had failed, both Charlie and John believed the idea feasible.

There were two dreamers now.

In February, 1906, when a new superintendent was needed

in the Zanesville mill, Tytus was promoted to that post on Hook's recommendation.

Pinning his faith to men, George Verity encouraged the use of imagination among his associates. Sitting at his desk, he developed methods for the assembly and organization of a tremendous amount of diverse information at his fingertips. In later years, there were two desks, a roll-top one for the storage of information less frequently required, and a large flat-topped one with its drawers crammed with filing systems and its working surface cluttered with today's problems. Near his right hand always lay a portfolio of his own design. A portable filing cabinet, its gaping mouths swallowed letters, memoranda and clippings requiring further rumination tonight or tomorrow. Snapped shut, it became an underarm reference library for the conference table, the Pullman compartment or the evening at home.

A voluminous filing system lay convenient in the bottom drawers of his two desks.

"By keeping data and information on tap, garnered as it comes across my desk or from books, magazines or other publications," he said, "I needn't bother busy people to look things up for me."

In addition, two tall slender cabinets with horizontally narrow shelves flanked his roll-top desk. They held valuable numbered scrapbooks, and the key to their amazingly diversified contents was a numbered list under the glass covering his flat-top desk.

An omnivorous reader and an inveterate wielder of editorial shears, he marked and clipped whatever he deemed significant, well-phrased or worthy of preservation. Often such clippings were routed to the desks of his associates with his comments or instructions written on an attached note.

"I do a lot of reading for the boys," he said. "They are usually too busy to do it themselves."

His "reading for the boys" was to have great effect upon an experiment which his associates launched in the second five-year period.

10

Carnahan Fights Corrosion

THE Curtis Street mill was now a buzzing hive. The expanded rolling capacity, created by taking over the Zanesville mill, taxed the Middletown open-hearth furnaces to their limit.

A legend grew—and persisted—that the excitable, energetic Carnahan used to respond to midnight crises in his department by leaping on a horse and riding hell-for-leather through the streets of Middletown, bellowing to his snoring crews to turn out and get to work.

"It's a lie!" said Orley Moles, Bob's fiercely devoted apologist, explaining that it all got started one night when Carnahan rode a horse through town, looking for an electrician because the power had failed, stalling a crane, just as a heat was being tapped.

But Orley never denied that there was a night when his helpers ducked out for a quick drink and failed to return, and that he ran out into the street, grabbed a peg-legged man by the collar, dragged him inside and put him to work as a helper.

"He was a good one, too!" said Orley. "Sober and reliable and a lot better than some two-legged tramps I could name without half trying."

For Orley, who didn't lean on a bottle for his strength,

"weaklings" was the word for those brawny men who fortified themselves with strong waters for the grueling twenty-four-hour turns which were the regular diet of steelworkers once a fortnight in those years of the twelve-hour-day, seven-day week.

Orley had been tempted to quit when Strawbridge left and invited him to come along.

"He made me a good offer, too!" he said. "But I thought it all out and decided I wouldn't go because here, if you had a grievance, you could take it to Mr. Verity and he'd listen and try to understand even if your complaint was silly. Besides, I couldn't let Mr. Carnahan down. He needed me. When he was trying to work out some new way of making steel, he'd take me to his desk and I'd sit beside him while he figured and asked me what I thought of his ideas. He said I had the furnace knowledge he needed and as he had all the book learning, each of us seemed to have what the other needed."

Old-timers aver that, in all the years he was a melter, Orley never spoiled a heat or burned a furnace. They say his knowledge of the boiling iron brew's composition was so uncannily perfect that he could determine, by peeping into the inferno, almost exactly what chemical analysis would show up later.

Like his hero, Orley called the open-hearth department "home." The furnaces were his wives—wives whose temperaments he understood and for whose whims he made allowances. He cajoled, coddled, wooed and browbeat them as circumstances dictated. He was a man to shun in those nerve-taut moments when one of his furnaces began to labor in the heat of gestation, for he was then a husband beside himself with soul-tearing agony while "she"—as he called each one of them—gave birth to her roaring and hissing spawn. Even into his old age, his proudest boast was:

"I never hurt a-one of 'em—*ever!*"

For the devotion of these two men to each other, to their work and to him, George Verity was to be deeply indebted in this second five-year period of the company's history; for, as the period began, the company was preparing for another adventure in pioneering—this time, a contest with steel's greatest menace—corrosion.

As the first five years of the twentieth century ended, mankind was poised for a mighty forward leap in the conquest of space. In the span of the preceding century, land miles and sea miles, which had remained stable for thousands of years, had been minimized mightily by steam and electricity, with metal ships and rails and wires.

Forces now emerging were to dwarf that marvelous century's amazing accomplishments. Orville and Wilbur Wright had just flown; the first wireless signal had just crossed the Atlantic; man was getting set to wreck all previous concepts of time and space.

Sea miles were being shortened: the Panama Canal was becoming a reality; the first cable across the Pacific carried a message that circumnavigated the formerly huge planet in only twenty-one minutes.

Land miles were being reduced: the first New York subway was completed; a photograph was transmitted marvelously over wire; the human voice had been carried across space without wires; a Philadelphia & Reading Railroad train had set a speed record of 115.2 miles per hour; a Packard automobile had crossed the United States under its own power; Henry Ford had driven his racing automobile a mile in 39.4 seconds and, having experimented to his own satisfaction, had launched a company with the aim of making automobiles cheap, serviceable, in quantity, for plain people.

Such was the setting at that moment, when, at last, nomadic man was getting set to heave himself free of the hampering mud of land miles that had held him for centuries.

But, where were the roads for these proposed automobiles?

"Reading for the boys," George Verity watched the signs and portents of the rapidly changing times, marked and clipped and annotated the reports and sent them around the circle of his associates.

"Look into this!" or "Watch that!" said the little notes, signed "G.M.V." attached to the clippings.

There was a report:

> "The United States Government Office of Road Inquiry is being reorganized as the Office of Public Roads, a bureau of the Department of Agriculture. Dr. Allerton S. Cushman will be in charge. One of the first acts of the bureau will be a census of American roads."

And later:

> "It has been revealed that, although a total of $79,595,-418 was spent last year on road improvements, only 153,662

of the nation's 2,151,590 miles of rural roads merit the term 'improved'."

The problem of improving roads through the use of better drainage wrinkled the brows of a little group of men who met in a hotel in Defiance, Ohio, in the fall of 1904. The day was gloomy but its murk was a sunny morning in May compared with the gloom of these men. For they were manufacturers and distributors of corrugated galvanized iron culverts which, though unquestionably ideal for highway drainage, were being scorned by highway improvers who scoffed:

"Tin cans! How long will they last underground?"

The question was not impertinent. These culvert manufacturers having no experience in the matter simply couldn't answer it. Nor could the manufacturers of sheet steel, upon whom the culvert manufacturers depended for their raw material. Nobody seemed to know the answer, and nobody—the road-builders least of all—wanted to make the necessary tests.

So here they were, these discouraged members of the Corrugated Iron Culvert Manufacturers Association, who had come to Defiance from their factories in Ohio, Michigan, Illinois and Indiana to discuss their dilemma with W. Q. O'Neal, the president of their association.

O'Neal, the operator of a culvert factory in Crawfordsville, Indiana, was the owner of the James H. Watson patents for making culverts by riveting corrugated galvanized sheet-steel "drums" together. The men gathered in that meeting were operating as licensees under his patents. They had paid him license fees for the privilege of manufacturing a highway-improvement device which highway builders refused to use. Mr. O'Neal was very much troubled over the whole trend of affairs.

At his desk in Middletown, George Verity read of this meeting up in Defiance and, reaching for the ever-ready shears, snipped out the clipping and handed it to his vice president in charge of sales, George H. ("Bert") Charls.

"Better attend this convention, Bert, and see what these fellows are doing," he said.

Charls attended the session and listened to many inquiries and lamentations. Then he arose and offered help. "While our company has had no previous experience in this matter," he said, "it is unquestionably interested in this important problem of corrosion, and we shall be happy to make whatever investigations and tests are necessary to secure the information required."

As simply as that, Armco was launched into investigation of the whole broad subject of corrosion of iron and steel of different grades under varying conditions of service.

In that investigation, Carnahan proved to be the spearhead of experimentation.

The first finding in the investigation was that steel, especially Bessemer steel, though tougher than iron, was actually inferior to iron wherever corrosion was the chief problem.

Nobody knew why. It was one of those "simply obvious" things which are neither simple nor obvious.

In its natural state, *iron is rust.* Left to itself, it is not particular about the company it keeps, therefore it is seldom pure. Of all companions, it likes oxygen best, and since oxygen is abundant almost everywhere on this planet, iron finds its favorite companion and becomes iron oxide or rust.

In its most useful industrial form, it is a product solely of man's ability to reverse a natural process through the use of heat. That is, in attempting to prevent iron from doing what it most wants to do, man has to rob other organisms of stored energy by applying his skeleton key—fire.

So the contest with corrosion is eternal, and the rate of man's success is measured by the sum total of thermal units he can filch from the solar radiation stored in forest trees, the fossilized sun energy hoarded in the dead organisms that are coal and petroleum, or the sun-lifted waters falling through hydroelectric sluiceways.

It has been estimated that, in the time required to wrest one ton of iron from rust with borrowed sun energy in furnaces, about five hundred pounds of serviceable iron reunites with oxygen into rust. There is, therefore, not much of a barrier between man and a dearth of serviceable iron. If the furnace fires should be allowed to go out for one century, there would be little evidence left in the world that man had ever learned how to tear iron and oxygen asunder.

The very existence of the frail barrier is contingent upon the feeding of those fires—plus man's recently developed ingenuity in learning to prevent iron from obeying the natural law of corrosion.

These are the basic issues in the long war of the human race against rust, the two major battlefields in the combat against corrosion.

Upon the second battlefield—the prevention or retarding of corrosion—the Verity strategists now sallied forth in the second five-year period of Armco history.

A convention of metal culvert manufacturers thrust George Verity and his associates into this war with rust. The clew that led to the final victory was a ridiculously common thing—a piece of wire.

Tremendous is the drama in a piece of wire. Hand-hammered as long as 3,600 years ago, it was feminine adornment mainly until as recently as 1350, when a Nuremberger named Rudolf mastered the trick of pulling a hot iron rod through a hole in a metal plate and, keeping the art secret, set up a virtual wire monopoly for himself and his descendants for almost two hundred years.

By 1630 the English mastered the trick, and thirty-five years later the process came to America. Largely because of the increasing cheapness of wire, which it used liberally, the mechanized textile industry was able to set the stage for the Industrial Revolution.

In 1831, when mechanization of the textile industry sent Grandfather Matthew Verity to America, John Roebling also came over to farm and, later, to spin wires into river-spanning bridges. That year, too, Michael Faraday wound two wires on a bar of iron, and Ichabod Washburn, a Massachusetts textile maker, set up his own wire mill. Ichabod probably thrilled as much as Samuel F. B. Morse when the words, "What hath God wrought?" flashed electro-magnetically along a strand of wire.

Certainly it was a great day for his mill, the nation's principal producer of wire, when Lincoln signed the Homestead Law which offered free land out of the public domain to anyone who would cultivate it, for, in 1865, thousands of men shucked military accouterments to beat swords into plows and till free acres in the West—and created a tremendous market for wire.

Barbed wire, invented within the next decade, was the answer to the need for fence in the treeless, stoneless western plains. The hand-fashioning of barbed wire was a boyhood chore for the Illinois neighbor farm boys Elbert H. Gary and John W. Gates, and from Gates's early successes as a barbed-wire salesman the United States Steel Corporation may be said to have stemmed.

Alluring, indeed, are the dramatic aspects of wire's story, but what is of most moment to George Verity's story is the fact that wire, being light and thin, is a perfect medium for the consuming passion of iron for oxygen.

Corrosion was not much of a problem as long as single strands of barbed wire fenced the farms, for this early Bessemer steel wire was so cheap that it was easily patched or replaced. Woven-wire fence, invented in 1884 by the Michigan farmer, J. Wallace Page, brought the problem of corrosion to the fore.

By 1900 the value of wire fence enclosing American farms was estimated at $3,830,000,000, and the lust of iron for oxygen was whittling the value down so fast that the United States Department of Agriculture hired a chemist in 1901 and put him to work on a study of the corrosion of steel wire.

This chemist was born in 1867 in Rome, where his father was

American consul. Returning to America, where his father became an ironmonger in St. Louis, Missouri, he attended Worcester Polytechnic Institute and then, after studying at Freiberg and Heidelberg, and teaching at Bryn Mawr, he entered government service. Because he possessed a burning curiosity about the process of corrosion, he conducted exhaustive research on wire fence. In 1905, just after his superiors appointed him head chemist of the newly organized Office of Public Roads, this man, Dr. Allerton Seward Cushman, published his findings in Farmers' Bulletin No. 239.

This pamphlet fell on George Verity's desk mainly because he, the urban industrialist, had never lost his attachment to the farm and its problems.

It is a strange circumstance, indeed, that this report of Dr. Cushman's research, undertaken for the benefit of farmers, should have been published after he had assumed supervision of the chemical problems incidental to construction of public roads.

Why does steel corrode more rapidly than iron? The Cushman bulletin submitted no reasons. Until then, all progress in wresting iron from rust had been hit-and-miss, and had piled up by trial and error one of those collections of definitions and rules which, miscalled "knowledge," are merely fig leaves draping the nakedness of ignorance.

Mineralogy and metallurgy were sciences, of sorts. The word "metallography" had been coined, but the infant science had a name before it was conceived.

Metallurgists assumed that steel's more rapid corrosion was

due to the fact that it is an alloy—a combination of many elements with iron. Whether made in the Bessemer converter or the open-hearth furnace, it might contain such impurities as sulphur, phosphorus, silicon, carbon, manganese, copper and other minerals, plus certain gases. All of these, they added, might be controlled to some extent in melting and annealing. The explanations were detailed, but the questioners wryly observed that the experts called a lot of valuable things "impurities."

"What is the relation of these so-called impurities to the rate of corrosion?" the Verity associates asked.

No answer.

"We'll find the answer," said Carnahan.

They were conditioned for the search. They had been told in 1900 that you couldn't galvanize basic open-hearth steel and, being stubborn enough to doubt, had done "the impossible." They had been told that it would be unprofitable to make sheet steel with controlled magnetic quality and, doubting that too, were now doing it with profit to themselves, the electrical industry and the public. They were being told that steel's tendency to corrode fast was the price one had to pay for steel's superior strength, and, with George Verity backing them up and prodding them on, they were saying, "We don't believe that either!"

Troublesome creatures, doubters! Flealike, they believe not at all in letting sleeping dogs lie, so they nip the lazy flanks of human inertia and the race scratches itself frantically and thereby makes what is called "progress."

When that bulletin of Dr. Cushman's fell on the Verity

desk and was passed to Charls and Carnahan with the customary little white flag marked, "Look into this—G.M.V." it was heartening for the active doubters to find they were not alone.

From Verity to Cushman went a letter:

> "We are eager to learn all we can about this subject of corrosion. If you can suggest any improvement in the accepted analyses of steel from which fence and thin sheets are made, we will be glad to try them out."

Thus began a close collaboration with Dr. Cushman, who was awarded the Franklin Medal a year later, and who continued thereafter as Armco's special consulting chemist.

Dr. Cushman believed that steelmaking processes could and should be revised so as to eliminate or reduce the so-called impurities which constituted the points of attack for corrosion. Steelmakers said the reductions recommended were impracticable. Carnahan said they might easily ruin the furnaces.

Sales Manager Charls, who had become the guide and inspiration of the culvert manufacturers, urged Verity to issue an order to the effect that the experimentation should go on. He said, "We can well afford to risk the loss of a furnace in an experiment so far-reaching in its importance as is this study of corrosion."

Orders were given and the risk was taken.

New trials began in 1905. Again and again Carnahan and his assistants tried to reduce the particular elements being attacked to the points desired. Again and again they failed.

There were enough little encouragements from time to time to make them willing and anxious to go on trying.

There's no telling what sort of a ride you'll get when you sink the hooks of a few question marks into the hide of that blundering beast called "impossible." You may be yanked into a direction not in your plans at all. That's what happened in this case. The first thing these rash experimenters knew, they were actually going down hill backward—completely reversing established steelmaking processes by deliberately oxidizing baths of molten metal in the furnaces to burn out those impurities.

What Carnahan was striving for was a reduction of manganese content to below .2 per cent with less than .04 per cent carbon. He demanded so many analyses of metal taken from the furnaces that he almost drove Gus Ahlbrandt, the young open-hearth chemist, frantic.

By December, 1906, this had been done so successfully that the culvert manufacturers, hearing Charls's report on progress to date, at a meeting in Crawfordsville, applauded the result.

Carnahan was then instructed to attempt to reduce the manganese content still lower, but the resultant waste of sheet bars broken in the mill prohibited the immediate continuation of the attempt. At the insistent demand of the management, Carnahan and his associates scrapped everything they thought they had learned about this problem and tackled it anew.

They now began at the raw-material piles where they carefully selected both the ore and scrap to be used, as they had done in preparation for the manufacture of electrical steel. They charged these selected materials into the furnaces and did deliberately what experienced steelmakers had always avoided—oxidized the metal bath to burn out the carbon and manganese. This required temperatures as high as 3,100 degrees and melting periods as long as thirteen hours. The injury to furnace and ladle linings was frightful. Company records of the period bristle with notations of shut-downs caused by liquid steel cutting through furnace walls into slag pockets and whole heats of metal boring through the bottoms of ladles.

Orley Moles almost wept over his injured furnaces. Then, though he did all in his power to coddle and protect them, one of them almost became his undoing. "But it wasn't her fault!" he said afterward.

On January 27, 1907, Orley made a trip down into the subterranean chambers of a furnace to see about drying out some accumulated dampness. One of the helpers had forgotten to turn off a gas valve. As Orley reached the bottom of Number Two furnace under repair, the heat from Number One, then operating, ignited the trapped gas. Next thing Orley knew he was on top of the furnace.

When he gained consciousness, he was—as he put it—"as nekkid as a new-born 'possum." When they picked him up, his leg, he said, "slithered around like a dying snake."

They wanted to amputate his leg. George Verity summoned the best surgeons in the area as consultants, but Orley fought them off. He'd be damned if he'd come out of it a cripple, he said. He'd die rather than do that. But he didn't die and he didn't come out of it a cripple.

Carnahan visited him twice every day and told him over and

over, in that gruff but appealing manner of his, that "by jove and by gad, you'd better get well and whole if you know what's good for you. We simply cannot carry on our experiments without your help."

Orley's injury was a serious handicap to the experimenters. A greater setback was coming.

Life seemed comfortably safe in the evening of October 21, 1907. Business was booming; men were at work regularly; wages were improving; every prospect pleased. Even the seas were going to be safe now, for the first wireless message had crossed the Atlantic three days before, and a fine new steamship, the largest passenger liner in the world, a practically unsinkable palace, was steaming serenely eastward after having made a record-breaking crossing on her maiden voyage to New York. She was the *Lusitania.*

Then, mysteriously out of the nowhere, during the night, a great fear struck New York.

Before dawn of the twenty-second, scores, then hundreds, and later, thousands of fear-crazed people lined up before the Knickerbocker Trust Company in Manhattan. They had been brought there by a rumor that the bank was in danger of failure. The run on the bank continued all day and precipitated runs on other banks all over the United States. By noon of the twenty-third the Knickerbocker directors suspended payments because their cash was nearly exhausted, and the currency panic of 1907 was on in full fury, toppling banks, wrecking industries, causing untold human misery.

II

Panic

TO FOLK who dwell along Middletown's Main Street, autumn is the year's most welcome season. Paralleling the river, the street lies on the stream's broad flood-plain upon which summer's heat is the breath of a forge.

The tall clock in the hall at 230 South Main Street struck five when George Verity, ready for his daily horseback ride, stepped from his side-porch door into the crisp coolness of an October dawn. The formal garden, which he and Mrs. Verity had planned and built in the small back yard, was deeply carpeted with fallen leaves. He waded through the crackling, golden flood, stepped through a gap in the garden's surrounding hedge and walked out upon a broad expanse of clipped turf. This, he remembered happily, had been an unsightly, weed-grown field beyond a trash-littered alley before he had bought it, added it to his yard and converted it into a playground for his children and their neighborhood companions. For a moment he stood, surveying the silent yard, thinking of the wealth of remembered happiness with which its creation had rewarded him. Watching Main Street's tall maples relinquish their yellow leaves, one by one, he thought:

"Like gold slipping from the fingers of dying misers."

He walked across the playground and stepped through another hedge onto a larger field lying on a lower level of the floodplain. Surrounded by tall trees which screened it from the dismal chaos of squatters' shacks in the bottomlands to the north of his property, this was the Verity "farm yard"—the site for stable and pasture for his horses and Mrs. Verity's cow.

He saddled his riding horse and rode out. On his way into the country, he halted for a brief pause near the site of Middletown's new high-school building upon which construction was beginning.

A year ago he had consented finally to his neighbors' demands and had become a member of the school board. His first official act was to assist in the planning of this school.

"It looks like an awful lot of money!" the more timid members of the board said when it was proposed that a bond issue for the required $84,000 be laid before the public for a vote. Though the bond issue had been passed by the narrow margin of only three votes, the school was now being built.

"The building of this school ought to be the beginning of a better spirit of co-operation in Middletown," the new board member had said to his friend Harlan.

An hour later he returned for breakfast. At seven o'clock he arrived at the plant "to get a lot of work done before others come and interruptions begin." He entered, as usual, by a back gate which some of the workmen used. Spying a tangle of rusting cable lying too close to the bar-mill entrance for safety, he summoned a man working in the yard and said:

"Someone might trip over a loop of that cable and get hurt. I think it ought to be moved, don't you?"

"Yes, sir," the man replied. Charlie, an electrician, who had followed him through the gate, saw him talk to the yardman and then proceed to the office.

Walking over to the yardman, Charlie said:

"New around here, ain't you, Bud?"

"Yeah," said the yardman. "Why?"

"Thought I'd give you a tip."

"Yeah?"

"Yeah," said Charlie. "Know who that was you were just talking to?"

"No. . . . Who?"

"Mr. Verity, president of this outfit."

"Yeah?"

"Yeah."

"Friendly, ain't he?"

"Yeah. . . . What'd he say to you?"

"Said he thought somebody might get hurt falling into that mess of cable yonder and asked me if I didn't think it ought to be moved."

"You going to move it?" Charlie asked.

"Who? Me!" said the yardman. "Why should I move it? It ain't my job. Besides, he didn't give me no orders to move it. Only asked me if I didn't think it ought to be moved."

"Listen, Bud!" said Charlie. "Mr. Verity don't give orders to nobody—never! He ain't built that way. If he sees what he thinks ain't right, he asks you if you don't think it ought to be made right. If you say yes, like you just did, *that's* your orders. Gives you a chance to use your noodle, he does. And he don't ever forget it if you use it. You can take my tip or leave it, Bud; but if I was you I'd move that cable."

At his desk, George Verity unfolded the morning newspaper, glanced at the front page and whistled sharply. The news was bad. The run on the Knickerbocker Bank in New York, spreading fear throughout the land, was becoming a nation-wide panic.

But, what was this?

Out of the columns of type reporting the devastation of this tidal wave of fear, one fact leaped, hit him hard and left him dizzy.

"It can't be true!" he said, looking again at the report that the Westinghouse Electric & Manufacturing Company had sought a receivership.

It was a black moment in this small steel company's history when, Verity's associates having been summoned and the news item reviewed, the full significance of the Westinghouse situation was apparent to them, for, from this great electrical manufacturer, one of Armco's best customers, the unsuspecting Verity associates had for several months past accepted "commercial paper" instead of cash in settlement of monthly statements. The company's books disclosed a paper claim of $160,000 against Westinghouse. The loss of such a sum—ten per cent of Armco's invested capital—would be potentially ruinous.

"Men," said Verity, quietly, "we cannot stop to cry over

this announcement. We must get the facts and try to see what can be done."

To this little band of pioneers, living and working in a small midwestern community, the Westinghouse Company was a tower of strength—an industrial giant that could not fail. There *must* be some mistake!

So Verity began an investigation of Westinghouse history. The very first thing he learned was that this was the third time the company had been in receivership. This startling discovery called for further, more complete investigation.

A trip to New York disclosed that the electrical company's financial difficulties were due entirely to the fact that George Westinghouse, though a great inventive genius, was so deeply absorbed in his research developments that he had little concern for the financial problems involved in his growing enterprise.

"The outstanding success of his revolutionary air-brake invention and his far-seeing grasp of the problems and possibilities in the electrical industry had started him out on a promotional program which included the development of manufacturing plants in several European countries," reported Verity.

"These plants, new and growing and operating at long range, together with his air-brake and electrical business at home, were demanding new capital faster than he could provide it.

"The difficulty was apparently due to too rapid expansion while deeply engrossed in new developments. He had but little respect for the sensitive nature of financial institutions and the investing public.

"He was just too busy to bother about financial problems

and he did not have any active partners or associated officials with either the experience or strength to influence him in such matters."

Verity reported all this to his company's board of directors, adding his conviction that the business of the Westinghouse Company itself was sound and likely to have a great future if provided financial management suited to the needs of the courageous inventor.

"It is now simply a question of what, if anything, we can do to help," he added.

Verity's inquiry disclosed that Westinghouse had prepared a plan for the financial readjustment of his company as a counter to a plan announced by a large group of creditor institutions in the financial district.

The bankers' "Readjustment Plan," as it was called, was so drastic that it would have eliminated the common-stock interests and left the company's future in the hands of bankers.

Verity's associates suggested that he call on Westinghouse and offer his personal services and those of the company in support of Westinghouse's own plan for reorganization.

George Westinghouse greeted George Verity most warmly and discussed freely his company's affairs and his plan. Finally he said:

"If you really want to assist me, how would you like to interview some of our largest merchandise creditors, explain my plan to them as you understand it, and see if they are inclined to support it?"

Verity promptly undertook the mission by interviewing the

ten largest creditors who, together, held very large claims against the company.

Within a comparatively short time he succeeded in getting that group into the inventor's office for a conference which resulted in the official organization of the "Merchandise Creditors Committee" in support of Westinghouse's plan.

Verity was elected secretary of a subcommittee of that group. Furnished a desk in the company's New York offices, he worked for a year on the problem of securing creditors' consent to the plan.

He endeavored to spend every fourth week at home; however, he was not always able to do this, for the task he had undertaken was made extremely difficult by the pessimism of the bankers, who predicted flatly that it could not be done.

In spite of such opposition the committee of merchandise creditors secured sufficient consents to make the plan operative. Meantime, Westinghouse himself had done the "impossible" in obtaining a large amount of new capital from his old stockholders.

Ultimately the company was reorganized with a directorate, chosen half from the bankers' group and half from the merchandise creditors. Westinghouse was continued as president, and a board chairman was chosen and given power over financial operations, subject to the directorate's instructions.

Verity was one of the original directors. Serving continuously for some thirty-three years, he was, on January 1, 1941, the only survivor of that first directorate.

All foreign plants having been closed or disposed of, the reorganized company soon regained its stride, becoming one of the world's largest electrical manufacturers.

During his year in New York, Verity came to have a very high regard for the great inventive genius who was called "Uncle George" by his associates. At the end, when it came time for Verity to return to tasks at home, "Uncle George" wanted him to remain with him. But in the year he had been away from Middletown so large a part of the time, his own business had been pounded by the same forces of panic which had so nearly wrecked the Westinghouse Company.

That panic, based solely on fear, drove currency into hiding. Gold vanished entirely, legal tender was scarce, and many communities had to resort to scrip.

As the panic continued, Verity's associates urged him to return for a short time to help plans to meet the company's pay rolls.

Summoning the entire personnel of the company, Verity explained that the use of scrip could be avoided in the community if everyone had faith in his neighbor.

"I suggest that we all demonstrate our faith in one another by depositing our pay checks in the bank and drawing only such cash as we actually need," he said.

As a result, Middletown acquired fame in the area as the only town in which not one piece of scrip was issued.

In 1908, when he was again summoned to Middletown because the company's financial problems were becoming increasingly difficult, he was heartened and moved almost to tears by a fine demonstration of the men's faith in him. A group of sheet-mill men, rollers, roughers and heaters, aware of the company's difficulties, met in the union's lodge hall and voted to permit the company to withhold twenty dollars a month out of their pay as long as the money was needed. A committee reported the decision to Verity, and he could scarcely speak when he thanked them and said he would not accept their proposed sacrifice save as a last resort.

A few days later the mill re-echoed with cheers when secretary Phillips announced that a whopping big order had come in and that work could go on.

Throughout this year of unusual adversity the bonds between management and men were strengthened immeasurably. At one time, the management offered to turn its cost sheets over to a committee of workmen—an unheard-of thing in that time when, as Dennis Burrl Lauderback recalled, "there was no love lost between union men and their bosses in any other steel mill in the whole United States."

"Denny"—as he was called—was a roller and an official of the Amalgamated Association.

"It wouldn't be truthful to say there was never any trouble in the mill," he said. "There was—plenty of it! But it never went beyond the conference table. At that table we learned to look upon Mr. Verity and Charlie Hook as friends rather than as part of any opposition. I never heard Mr. Verity criticized at any labor convention I ever attended—and I attended a lot of them. That may not mean much nowadays, when organized labor generally has won a lot of the rights it was fighting for, but it meant a lot then, when most industrialists and labor organizers not only walked on opposite sides of the street but watched one another like hawks."

Yes, there *was* trouble in the mill—plenty of it! For, as financial skies cleared and orders increased, Carnahan, urged by Charls and encouraged by Verity, intensified his efforts to purify steel—and the devastation of material, equipment and men's dispositions was a repetition of what had happened during the electrical steel experiments—but played on a still grander scale.

12

Mill or Madhouse?

WHEN the threatened failure of the Westinghouse Companies took George Verity east for a prolonged stay, Carnahan and his associates in the open-hearth department were just beginning to feel the solid footing of achievement in their attempts to purify iron.

One by one they eliminated most of the chemical impurities which Dr. Cushman blamed for the rapid corrosion of steel.

It was not easy. The chronicles of the triumphs and failures, the heartaches and headaches—all of these became legends which are still embroidered by old-timers who participated in the battle.

Men, remembering their parts in the earlier attempt to make electrical steel, sometimes had to pinch themselves to make sure they were not dreaming.

There was more at stake now than there had been in the earlier experiments. Moreover, the entire industry was watching, for, when once you kick a hole in tradition, it becomes a place for peeping Toms to watch. The Toms, watching, said, "That isn't a mill—it's a madhouse!"

There were good reasons for the dictum, for, on the face of it, the experiments Carnahan was being asked to make, often against his own best judgment, looked like lunacy. As everybody knows, oxygen is what makes iron corrode—yet here was this practical and courageous steelmaker, being forced to attempt to purify iron by pumping it full of oxygen in the furnaces! It's crackbrained!

So said the outsiders.

Neither Verity nor Charls deemed it crazy. Verity continued to encourage it and silenced doubts by citing his faith in "individualism in thinking and co-operation in doing." "An unbeatable combination," he called it.

Neither Carnahan nor Moles now thought it crazy, for hard experience had worked its wonders before. Both were now married, but both were virtually living in the mill again.

Still it often looked like madness.

It is about as easy to oxidize a brew of iron as it is to scramble eggs, but the deoxidizing of the stuff, which had to be accomplished afterward, is a good deal like trying to unscramble an omelet. For, as they soon discovered, the oxidizing of the bath in the furnace left a lot of gas in the brew; and, when the stuff began to congeal in the molds, the ingots often belched. Sometimes they belched so lustily that there was nothing left in the mold but a thin shell. Such shells, light but resembling thousand-pound ingots, furnished amazement to visitors and amusement to mill hands who tossed them around in fake demonstrations of superhuman strength.

Even when the gas behaved in the molds, tiny gas pockets, hidden in the molten ingot, expanded in the sheet mills and the sheets would be laminated and worthless.

Or, if that did not happen, the gas would leak out of sheets and counteract chemicals in the galvanizing tanks, producing zinc blisters on the sheets—and causing Daniel Owen Fisher, the chief in the galvanizing department, to blister the atmosphere with his opinion of himself for having left his old man's farm in West Virginia. (Fisher came to Ohio in 1901 to work on a farm, arrived too late for the harvest, took a job in the mill "to earn enough to go home Christmas"—and never did go home.)

Many strange things were tried in attempts to eliminate the gas. Carnahan was forever experimenting to see what would happen. What usually happened was a frightening spectacle, according to shy Diltz Mitchell, who came to work in 1903 despite his widowed mother's fears about "man-killing steel mills." Diltz didn't dare tell his mother this:

"When one of these heats was tapped, the place was filled with fireworks, as hot steel exploded and men scampered for their lives. Above the roar and the crackle you could hear the yelling of Carnahan and Moles. Carnahan, always heaving things in the ladles, often got so excited that he jumped up and down and flung his own hat in. Sometimes it seemed he was on the point of throwing himself in too."

To Albert Hoppe, also, the experiments provided amusement and amazement. Al came up out of a coal mine in 1901 to become a rigger (maintenance man) for Armco. Working up among the rafters and beams, far overhead, he developed the agility of a monkey. He needed it, he recalled, ". . . when those guys prowled around down below with mysterious bundles under their arms. They'd slip up alongside a ladle when a heat was being tapped, and heave a bundle in. When they did, everybody would get the hell out of the way—fast. You never knew what'd happen. Sometimes the stuff would go *Whoosh!* right up to the ceiling. Once when it happened I was on the pouring platform. When Carnahan heaved a bundle in and the stuff began to bubble, I started running. A guy running ahead of me was going so fast I could have played checkers on his coat-tail."

To get rid of the gas, they tried stirring the brew with green wood. The results were so encouraging they denuded the area of saplings. When they couldn't lay hands on another young tree, they heaved in barrels until there wasn't a barrel in Middletown. Next they tried boxes and picked the town clean of kindling wood. They tossed in mill scale, cold iron, silicon—everything they could think of.

One combination blew the roof off a furnace. Another time an attempt to keep the brew in action after tapping was so eminently successful that the whole fifty-ton mess lifted itself right out of the ladle and sailed toward the roof.

Finally, largely by accident, Orley heaved a batch of aluminum shot into a heat in a desperate attempt to prevent another ascension of hot metal. It worked!

They tried it again and again, in the ladles and in the molds, a little of it and a lot of it, at the moment of tapping and at the moment of teeming—and, after much trial and error, they finally found out how much to add and when to add it.

There was a time when Orley worked ninety-six hours in one week beside Carnahan and then topped that off with an eighty-four hour stretch the next week, the two of them becoming hourly more tigerish in temperament as they wrestled with balky heats.

"Fun," they called it!

Echoes of this fun on the banks of the Big Miami reached the ears of young Leo F. Reinartz, a chemist at the J. Edgar Thomson mill in Pittsburgh. Leo liked what he heard—liked especially what he heard about George Verity's approval of such unorthodox experimentation. Investigating further, he learned that Armco needed a chemist. But, before he decided to go to Middletown, he called on his former chemistry teacher for advice.

"Middletown?" said the professor. "Oh, yes! I remember now. They're trying to make pure iron there. . . . Confidentially, my boy, they're crazy."

"Crazy, professor?"

"Yes, crazy."

"Then," said Leo, "do you advise me not to go?"

"On the contrary, my boy! It's possible that they may be crazy enough to succeed."

On July 5, 1909, Leo walked out Curtis Street to report for work as chemist in the open-hearth department. The sight he beheld when he stepped inside convinced him the professor's opinion had been right but his advice had been wrong. The furnaces were cold and threatening to collapse, and Carnahan, though far from cold, was also threatening to collapse. Furnaceman Bill Rupp had achieved his dubious distinction as "the only man who ever shut down all Armco operations."

Perhaps the only Armco man who never considered Bill Rupp's feat funny was William Otto Rupp, himself.

Bill was a Middletown boy who came to Armco in 1902 from a tobacco factory. When Strawbridge left in 1904 Bill went along. Two years later he was back, repentant. Since a third furnace was then being built, Orley took him under his wing as a helper. He learned fast and became such a reliable aid to Carnahan and Moles that, on July 4, 1909, the two of them overloaded him with responsibility.

Now, it was Carnahan's self-appointed duty to see to it that the furnaces were kept going over the holiday and brought up to melting temperature by the morning of the fifth. But Carnahan had an out-of-town engagement and delegated the duty to Orley.

But Orley had planned a trip too, so Bill got the assignment.

Early in the afternoon of the Fourth, Bill started for the mill. A friend of his hailed him on the street and invited him to a bricklayers' picnic in a cool grove in the country. Bill pondered the invitation. The town was a lonely place. The only movement on the streets was the shimmering of heat.

Cool grove . . . companionship . . . hot town . . . deserted mill, thought Bill.

"And lots of cold beer!" said his friend.

"I could stand a couple," said Bill, rasping his pebbly tongue against the roof of his mouth.

Next thing he knew he was in bed. People were shaking him and demanding why he hadn't gone to work.

"What time is it?" he asked.

"Nine o'clock," they said.

"Morning or evening? And what day?"

It was the morning of July 5, and Bill pulled the covers over his head and groaned.

"Carnahan wants to see you," they said.

Bill groaned. He didn't want to see anybody—ever.

But the messengers continued to come, and Bill decided he'd better go down and let Bob Carnahan throw him out with the customary words and music.

"I felt like a bad boy walking to a waiting angry papa in the woodshed," Bill said. "When I reached Carnahan's office he was very quiet and calm. 'Why did you do it, Bill?' he said. I thought I was done for, so I told him the truth, straight out. I had nothing to lose."

Then the unaccountable happened. Carnahan asked:

"Bill, what would *you* do to Bill Rupp if you were Bob Carnahan?"

Though he hadn't expected the question, Bill thought fast. "Well," he said, "I'd be tempted to kick him out of the place. But then I'd remember that he's been a pretty good man up to now, and I'd decide to be kind of easy on him for his first failure."

"That's not bad!" the quixotic Carnahan exclaimed, smiling suddenly.

Recalling it, Bill said, "It was the prettiest smile I've ever seen in my life!"

"You go home," said Carnahan, "and think this over for a week without pay. Then you come back and, if you behave, the whole thing will be forgiven and forgotten."

Bill came back and redeemed himself. Once he kept a heat at high temperature for more than twenty-four hours, without rest, while Carnahan supervised the helpers around the blocked taphole, sharing their risks and labors as they chopped and chopped at a "frozen monkey" and hoped they would be able to leap aside when their chisels should break through and release the volcanic flood.

He became a respected senior melter later. "But," he said, "though that affair was forgiven, I guess it will never be forgotten."

One night, shortly after chemist Reinartz started to work in this madhouse of a mill, he rubbed Carnahan the wrong way—an easy accomplishment. The eruptive Bob gave him the usual verbal garnishing, topped off with:

"You're fired! Get out of my sight!"

Leo trudged to his office and packed his belongings. He was an unhappy young man, for he was just beginning to like this crazy place. On the way out, he stopped to say good-by to Orley Moles.

"Where you going?" said Orley.

"Carnahan just fired me," Leo replied.

"Fired you!" said Orley. "Hell, that means he likes you! He's fired everybody around here hundreds of times. You go back to work and stay out of his sight for a few hours. In a little while, he'll cool off and come around to you and apologize."

Leo returned to work and kept out of Carnahan's sight for about a week. Then, one day, Carnahan spotted him.

"Where have you been, Leo?" he said. "I've been looking for you for a week. I wanted to apologize for flying off the handle the other night."

As he achieved mastery over this problem of purifying iron, Carnahan's disposition mellowed. The troubles were over—in the open-hearth department. In the mills they now began, for all the problems of rolling this material were new, manifold and complicated. Refractory clay, burned loose in the furnace department's equipment and imbedded in ingots, remained hidden until the sheet was rolled into a thing that was a steel-framed mud pie. "Clay-piped ingots," they called these.

They had first to learn the "critical" temperatures at which the stuff could be rolled. At times they rolled bars so hot that they dripped molten metal.

It was a great moment when they started the first "perfect" ingot through the mills. "It was a beautiful sheet," said James Richmond Byrum, who helped put it through the mill. James A. Pierce was selected to roll the first pack. "When Jimmy started rolling," said Byrum, "everybody dropped everything and come a-running to watch. It was a beautiful pack. We all stood around admiring it. Then the pack openers tackled it—and everybody groaned. The pack had welded itself into a solid slab."

Once more they had to experiment crazily, tossing such things as coal dust and sawdust between the doubled sheets to try to prevent "stickers."

One day a mill broke down just as a pack was ready to be passed through it. Before the mill was repaired the pack had cooled far below what was considered its proper temperature.

The teeming of a heat in the original Curtis Street plant: the young man at extreme left is Calvin Verity, now executive vice-president and general manager; man with left arm crossed over his chest is Earl A. Emerson, now president of Armco International Corporation; man pointing to ladle is G. F. Ahlbrandt, now assistant vice-president; man in white shirt just back of ladle is Charles R. Hook, now president.

The catcher on one of the old manual sheet mills.

"Let's put her through anyway, and see what happens," they said.

What happened was a pack of perfect sheets. Now they had mastered the whole process.

Application for patent was filed July 16, 1909, and granted and issued on the following November 23. Subsequently patents were taken out in every civilized nation.

They published their guarantee that their iron was 99.84 per cent pure, and other steelmakers said, "Horse-feathers!"

When they produced what they claimed they could, there were attempts at piracy that had to be settled in court. Then there were other tricks.

One night Orley had a visitor who came up to him while he was at work and said:

"Remember me, Hoke?"

The nickname "Hoke" had been fastened on Orley when he started in steel in Muncie, and he hadn't heard it since that time.

The visitor, who had been a mill hand in Muncie, was now, he explained, a steel company official. He asked Orley a lot of questions about this process of making pure iron, but Orley "just pretended to be green as a gourd."

"Then," said Orley, "he offered me $650 a month under a three-year contract if I'd join his company. I told him I'd stick with Carnahan and Mr. Verity even if he offered me three times what I was getting. A few nights after that he came back and told me he had it straight that the company was going to sack me as soon as the process was perfected. I thought it was a lie.

Then I learned he was Mr. Verity's guest, and it kept coming back to me that maybe he wasn't lying. So, next day, I went to Mr. Verity and asked him.

"I never said any words in my life I wanted to swallow so much as those. As soon as they were out, I saw how they hurt him. I felt like a skunk. He talked to me quietly, showing me why the doubt was put in my mind. 'Don't you see that these people want to use you and then get rid of you?' he said. 'I'm sorry,' I said, 'I'll stick with you come hell or high water.' Then he promised me that as long as he had anything to say about the company, I'd have a job."

Neither promise was ever broken.

At first they called this new product of theirs simply "special iron." A Chicago customer, sensing its importance, suggested it be called "Ingot Iron" because it was virtually pure iron in ingot form. Since, by this time, salesmen and customers had formed the habit of contracting the company's corporate title into "Armco," the product rapidly became world-famous as "Armco Ingot Iron."

They had no idea at the start that their attempts to reduce steel's tendency to corrode would lead to something which would revolutionize standards in the sheet-metal industry.

Originally, the product was intended for culverts and wire fencing. A year after they produced the first of it, Page and Armco were closely linked in co-operative research and Page-Armco fence began to spread all over the earth. In Australia it fenced one of the world's largest sheep ranches. At Durban,

South Africa, it served as a submerged barrier against sharks at a bathing beach. In East Africa, a sultan installed twenty miles of it, eighty-eight inches high, around his palace grounds and a neighboring village, as barrier against jungle beasts.

Until they produced this pure iron, wood had been almost universally used in irrigation flumes. After they perfected it, the United States Reclamation Service was able to abandon wooden flumes, and sheets of this iron reclaimed deserts and enabled cities to use water carried hundreds of miles from mountain reservoirs.

But culverts were the mainstay, and the expanding road-improvement programs following increased use of automobiles made the mainstay profitable. Eventually, increasing collaboration of the company and culvert manufacturers linked them all together.

Early it was found that this new iron had exceptional electrical conductivity compared with other ferrous metals. Then it was discovered that it had unusual electrical welding properties and great quantities were eventually used as welding wire and rod.

Its uses spread—to underground tanks and hot-water tanks in homes, to five-million-cubic-foot gas tanks and ordinary garbage cans, to roofs and sidings of factories and eavetroughs on houses, to railway cars and shingle nails, to docks and ships, to locomotive jackets and metal lath, to baby bathtubs and caskets, to the million and one things where the strength of iron is not sufficient if iron's weakness for oxygen is the enemy.

One of its most important uses was the most unexpected.

For, when they labored to perfect it, no great importance attached to the manufacture of porcelain-enameled ironware. True, there were enameled pots and pans in every home, but, with the exception of imported ware, the enamel chipped off readily and the steel rusted, and housewives tossed the derelicts on the dump and, damning the makers, bought new ones.

Then, entirely by accident, an Austrian enameler, working in a refrigerator factory in Michigan, ran short of standard sheet steel which he had been using, and tried a few sheets of this iron. He reported that its enameling qualities were astonishingly good.

Until then, little was known about commercial enameling practices and less was known about the base-metal requirements. The Austrian enameler's report launched the Verity associates into a thorough study of both. Within a year they were supplying carloads of special iron to the first refrigerator manufacturer of one-piece, porcelain-lined provision chambers. This special iron was designed to hold porcelain permanently and stay flat under the three successive firings required to fuse it.

Later, when home refrigeration in steel cabinets replaced the old wooden iceboxes, the Armco product became standard base-metal for these and the rest of the glistening, enameled steel household appliances in modern kitchens, bathrooms, laundry rooms.

In the end the persistent and heroic experimentation raised the standard of iron and steel-sheet products in the industry; and the trade-mark name of this, one of the most valuable products ever produced by the company, became such a common synonym for pure iron in the steel markets of the world that it was customarily written without capital letters.

"This product," said W. W. Sebald, who was then the company's only traveling salesman, and is today vice president and assistant general manager, "was the vehicle that enabled the company to get world-wide recognition. Until it was perfected, culvert manufacturing, for instance, was a more or less tin-shop product. Supplied with Armco assistance in research engineering and sales development it became a highly specialized industry which ultimately developed enormous culverts to replace steel bridges."

The course of the development, Sebald added, set the stage here for a continuing program of frictionless liaison between such customarily unfriendly units of industry as sales and production departments.

By 1909, it was becoming obvious to George Verity and his associates that they would soon need elbow room. Tonnage had crept up steadily, month by month. Earnings grew. Around the conference table, the Verity strategists pondered and planned. They concluded they would have to double capacity by crowding additional plant and equipment on the original Curtis Street site, restricted though the space was.

But, just as they were well along with plans in the blueprint stage, the sales of ingot iron and other products began multiplying so rapidly that they returned to the conference table and asked:

"What will we do if further expansion is necessary later?"

Until now, they had employed "small-mill practice," a procedure in which small ingots are broken into bars for rolling into sheets. In planning to expand, they realized there was no room on this site for a change-over to "big-mill practice," in which large ingots are "roughed down" in a huge blooming mill.

Mere doubling of capacity, they determined, would not enable them to make steel at costs comparable to those of competitors using big-mill practice. So they threw their plans away and began new ones.

On October 9, 1909, they announced their decision to build an entirely new plant on a new site. It would employ big-mill practice and be modern in all respects. It was a big step to take; for, even if they ran the proposed blooming mill at only half capacity, they would have to increase sheet finishing facilities three-fold. Could they market such a large increase in sheet-mill production? It might prove to be a hazardous step, but they felt they had to take it. There seemed to be no alternative.

When Verity announced the new plant would cost $3,000,000 and employ 1,200 men, almost a dozen communities offered sites.

Great was the jubilation in Middletown when he told members of the Business Men's Club that he favored his home town for this expansion. But, he added, there were some conditions existing in his home town which he believed could and should be corrected.

13

Experiments in Neighborliness

THE beginning of George Verity's more active participation in community affairs coincided with the improvement in his company's financial condition and the expansion of its operations into Zanesville. When the new high school, which he had urged should be built, was completed, he joined a small group of Middletonians who were urging the construction of a much-needed hospital.

Substituting action for talk, he and Harlan quietly planned the launching of a public nursing bureau. Carnahan and Hook joined them. Each man pledged ten dollars a month as his contribution to the project. After they got twelve other men to go along with them on that basis, they hired a nurse and set up the bureau.

"We all believed that our growing city should have a hospital," said Harlan, "but it was hard to get the idea accepted outside our little group. The people along Main Street had little understanding of or interest in the people in other parts of the town; and the people on the other side of the tracks had good reason to suspect any proposal coming from what they called the Main Street snobs. So it was Verity's idea that all talk of such a project should be deferred until at least the first step toward the goal of a nursing bureau could be made.

Verity's understanding of class antagonisms was far from academic. Such antagonisms existed in steel mills, where rollers and melters were aristocrats in their separate realms of activity and common laborers were "buckwheats" if they were rural Americans, or "hunkies," whether they came from Hungary, Serbia, Greece, Austria, or Italy. In his own mill he was constantly insisting that more humane treatment be accorded the "hunkies" whom he deemed prospective Americans.

Learning that these foreign-born laborers were unwelcome in the town's houses, he ordered bunkhouses built for them. Later, when the company could better afford it, neat cottages with landscaped grounds were provided.

He then converted the old Doty homestead on the banks of the canal into a Foreign Club as a social center and provided it with instructors to help the men become American citizens.

Though old-time labor bosses gloomily predicted such "coddling" would breed trouble, the trained workers were themselves disposed to believe that Verity was genuinely interested in these patient toilers from foreign lands.

They were impressed by his kindly treatment of the "hunkies." One man, then a workman but later a company official, recalled that this alone convinced him that "Mr. Verity was an extraordinary man." Said he:

"Around Homestead, where I got my early training in steel, it was common practice to herd these immigrants in company-owned board-and-batten shacks where they lived like beasts in filth, under the supervision of padrones who ran the houses. Their beds were never made because they were always occupied. As one crew got out of bug-infested bunks, another unwashed crew tumbled into them. When an emergency arose in the mill, foremen went to the company houses and hauled the weary men out with no regard for their condition. The men were driven brutally. Foremen were often beaten or stabbed by men who had just come from work and refused to return to the mills without rest. So it became custom for foremen to enter the houses accompanied by armed bullies.

"I well recall how amazed the labor foremen were when Mr. Verity announced such practices would not be tolerated here. They argued with him. They fairly swamped him with what they called good reasons. He let them talk themselves out. Then he said, 'We will *try* my way.' "

Big Bill O'Donnel, the Pittsburgh-trained head labor boss, almost unhinged his lower jaw with amazement when Verity told him he would be expected to knock on doors before entering hunkies' houses. It was perhaps the first time in his loquacious career that Bill was utterly speechless. Old-timers aver that he walked out of the Verity office and down the hall, dazed with unbelief, and that when he finally recovered from the stunning impact of what he had heard, the most his ordinarily word-handy tongue could master was:

"My God! It's a Sunday school!"

But Bill obeyed orders like a good soldier. He not only knocked on doors but removed his hat when he entered. And the fine way these foreign-born workmen responded to the more humane treatment was an endless source of amazement to him.

"Before long," said one veteran who watched the transformation, "Mr. Verity was offering cash prizes for the cleanest company houses and making us foremen do the judging. It was astonishing how cleanly these men became when they were properly encouraged. Next thing we knew they were bringing their families in from Europe. As new company houses were built to accommodate the families, they were placed in roomy yards in units of four. Each unit was provided with a community toilet, bath house, garden plot and children's playground. Mr. Verity continued his practice of paying out cash prizes for cleanliness and good appearance of the homes and grounds, and, little by little, these people became good neighbors, bought their own homes, attended classes at their Foreign Club, and became substantial citizens."

Within his own organization, men were getting used to George Verity as an experimenter in neighborliness. The advisory committee system of employee representation, called unsound five years previously, was proving itself, as was that other "visionary" project, the Armco Mutual Benefit Association.

But beyond the factory gates class conflicts continued. In an attempt to project beyond the gates the experiments in neighborliness now bearing fruit within the plant, he encouraged all employees to interest themselves in civic activities. In time, there was rarely a civic committee without its share of Armco people—men and women motivated by his belief that "individuals who make up a community cannot rise above the limitations which the community imposes upon them."

Their motives were often misinterpreted. People began to say, "Armco is trying to run this town." So many said it that, in the fall of 1909, it became a battle cry for the opposition that defeated a proposal to obtain a Carnegie library for the town.

"It was mutual distrust born of narrow political partisanship that prevented us from getting that library," said Harlan. "People actually bragged about having voted against it just to show Armco who was boss."

Harlan recalled he was "fighting mad about this display of spite."

"But," he said, "Verity wasn't even angry. He said, 'Harlan, it's really our fault. We've been trying to sow good seed on concrete. We'll have to prepare the ground first. So many people have been so consistently ill-used that they are naturally suspicious of anyone who offers to help them. We must first convince them that we have no ulterior motives.' "

Late in December, after many Middletonians had been wondering about the conditions he had referred to in his conference with the Business Men's Club a short time ago, he called together nearly three hundred of his fellow citizens for a heart-to-heart discussion of the community's needs.

Pointing out that the company's decision to expand operations would undoubtedly result in a 30 per cent increase in the town's population, he warned that such an increase could be troublesome and costly unless thorough preparation were made to care for the needs of about five thousand additional residents.

"What is Middletown going to do with so large an increase in population in so short a time?" he asked. "Where are they to live in a city already short of homes? Where are their children to be educated? How are they to be entertained, intellectually, physically, socially?"

Citing the city's needs—more and better housing, better protection of life and property, greater school facilities, a public library, improved transportation equipment, a hospital, parks and playgrounds, better facilities for social activities, recreation and entertainment—he added:

"I feel it would be criminal if this great increase in population were permitted or encouraged, and civic and municipal needs allowed to take care of themselves."

All he asked for the company was assurance that the new plant's needs for such things as water supply and sewage disposal would be met. As a citizen, he urged his fellow townsmen to co-operate in the creation of a community of which they could be proud. Solemnly pledging that his company would do its full part, he received assurance that the municipality and all civic organizations would strive to build a better Middletown.

After a site for the new plant, ample for all possible future expansion, had been secured on the eastern outskirts of the city, the Verity associates' original fears about the financing of the expansion were found to have been unjustified. The underwriting of securities necessary to finance the new project was promptly accomplished.

On a brisk March day in 1910, George Verity, members of his management staff, and a score of friends trudged across the furrows of a cornfield and thrust a spade into the thawing ground to begin the construction of the great East Works. When operations began eighteen months later, it was already clear that fears about the difficulity of marketing the added output had been groundless. Indeed, while the new plant was being built, sales mounted so steadily that it was decided to continue operating the original mill to care for the increasing demands.

To help design and construct the East Works sheet and jobbing mill, John Tytus was brought back from Zanesville. When the big plant was completed he was made superintendent of its sheet-mill division.

The operating problems involved in this larger, more modern mill were many and varied. They brought sharply to the fore the need to give serious thought to a subject about which general superintendent Hook had carried on many discussions lately with members of his enlarged staff. That subject—"the employer's responsibility for safety"—bordered dangerously on industrial heresy in that time.

Until 1910 industry had not progressed far in the conservation of human effort. Factories and mills were dirty, dark, dangerous. Cheap labor came in a steady stream from Europe; therefore, few employers concerned themselves about labor-saving machinery. To waste labor was considered no waste at all. Workers took risks as a matter of course. Any man who balked at the risks involved was "soft." Minor accidents were common. Serious accidents were frequent. Hours were long and workers were usually too weary to be careful around dangerous equipment. The common concept of a steel mill as an "inferno," prevalent still, is a belated mirroring of a time when no insurance company would risk a group policy covering lives of steel workers—a time when fatalities in the mills along Chicago's "Cinder Shore" were so numerous that a fabulous "undertakers' war" broke out in the neighborhood.

"Many mills were absolutely unfit for human occupation," said George Verity. "I remember a story that was generally believed by the men in one city, to the effect that a large mill maintained a hospital far inside the plant. It was commonly told, with a shudder, that when a man was seriously hurt he was rushed there—and never came out. It was all a figment of some feverish imagination—but men believed it."

In 1910 Superintendent Hook decided to find out if the appalling accident rate could not be reduced. Working through the employees' advisory committee system, he encouraged the organization of a central safety committee. Under it, separate plant committees were formed and safety contests for cash prizes were instituted among competing departments.

The method worked. Men who had scorned safety measures as evidence of softness, willingly adopted them when encouraged by cash awards.

Thus the Verity associates were among the first to organize an active and continuing campaign against the toll of injury and death caused by industrial accidents. The innovation is significant when projected against the background of the history of industrial safety.

As early as 1902 Maryland enacted the first workmen's compensation law. Though it did not cover all industries or even all employees in specific industries, it was fought by a manufacturers' lobby and ruled unconstitutional.

Advancement of the cause of industrial safety was largely due to President Theodore Roosevelt's sensitive adaptability to public demands for reform. Such demands were shaped by the writings of men and women whom Roosevelt called "muck-rakers," writers who turned from revelations of corruption in politics to the spotlighting of greed and stupidity in big business. When one of them revealed shocking conditions in the meat-packing industry, Roosevelt rode the wave of public indignation and demanded both pure food and better working conditions from that industry.

On January 31, 1908, he proposed workmen's compensation for Federal employees. When the law was passed under President Taft, the minority groups in the states who had been fighting for industrial safety renewed their efforts. And, though it is no credit to their intelligence, it is a matter of record that many employers spent large sums on lobbies and propaganda in attempts to defeat these innovations which, after their adoption, redounded to their profit.

It is often said that the steel industry was the worst offender in this matter of work hazards, but seldom remembered that this industry actually began the movement toward industrial safety.

In 1907, almost a year before Roosevelt started shouting for reform, the Association of Iron and Steel Electrical Engineers was formed, and set up, at its first meeting, a safety committee to study the new hazards introduced into steel mills by the increased use of electricity. This was probably the first industrial safety committee in the United States.

Then, in 1909, a New York state commission published a startling set of findings. Investigating 20,000 cases of industrial accidents resulting in 2,000 deaths and 4,000 permanent injuries, the commission found that only about a quarter of the claims had brought payment. It revealed that where employers resorted to insurance companies to protect themselves against damage claims, the employees recovered damages in only 8 per cent of the cases.

Publication of this report stimulated the enactment of workmen's compensation laws by the states in 1911.

Meantime, Superintendent Hook had launched his company's private war on work hazards. Two years after he began it, he was able to report encouraging results when the Iron and Steel Electrical Engineers invited him to attend their famous Milwaukee meeting which was the world's first safety congress and the origin of the National Safety Council.

For full significance of this pioneering, statistics speak eloquently. In 1913, when the program began to become nationwide in scope, 35,000 died in industrial accidents in the United States. By 1937, though total employment had multiplied many times and industrial mechanization introduced millions of new hazards, the total had fallen to 19,500.

Nowadays, industrial hazards are measured according to "frequency rate," i.e., the number of lost-time accidents per million man-hours of work. By that yardstick, the Verity associates' pioneering was so effective that, by 1917, Armco became the first company in the iron and steel industry qualified to insure its employees under a group policy. Subsequently they pulled their frequency rate down from 31.2 in 1922 to 4.0 in 1930 and held it down.

In George Verity's concept of a man's responsibility to his fellowman, the attempt of an employer to protect his employees from accidental injury was good—but not good enough. He insisted that an employer's responsibility to his employees did not end with mere accident protection.

He talked of "the employer's responsibility for the employees' health and physical fitness," and his critics again muttered about his "visionary ideas."

Hitherto management had concerned itself not at all about the health of individual workers. Its attitude was that a man could stand a job or he couldn't, and if he couldn't, the remedy was simple—fire him!

"This whole plan of operation is wrong!" Verity said. "Naturally, under such conditions, the man who combines brawn and brain pits his wits against those of his employer. Their interests are antagonistic, and just as the employer strives to give as little wages for a day's labor as he can, so the workman in turn strives to give as little and as poor work for his day's pay as he can, and hold his job.

"How foolish it is to expect an indifferent workman—a man who looks upon his employer as his enemy—to take an active interest in his employer's machinery, materials or products!

"If a man lives in a dirty, unsanitary house, if he is only a day or so ahead of the bill collectors, if he knows that when he dies his widow and children will be helpless, is it unnatural that he should blame his employer? Feeling that way, what real motive has he for being anything but indifferent, if not worse, to his employer's property and profits?"

His attitude, expressed in an interview with a magazine writer who had come to Middletown to seek "the golden key" to his success in maintaining peace between management and men in those times of industrial dissension, does not seem strange nowadays, but it was considered so then.

"I should be foolish did I even intimate that we have found a 'golden key' that will unlock the puzzle of human differences and labor disputes," he said. "No such key will ever be discovered, I fancy, until all men are made over. But I can justly say we have found a way of living and working happily together. Our rate of labor turnover is low. Employees are slow to leave us. And we gather together and keep a high quality of men."

He insisted that "altruism" and "philanthropy" and "humanitarianism" were the wrong words for what he was recommending. A man's health, he said, is definitely important to his employer because a healthy man is more valuable than a sick one.

So, when plans for the new East Works had been drawn up, provisions were made for the small beginnings of what shortly became a completely equipped hospital. And, remembering workmen's unreasoning fears of plant hospitals—a relic of days when gruesome tales of hidden victims were told and believed—he ordered the building erected in plain sight of all, just outside the main entrance to the plant.

It has now become common practice for industries to maintain first-aid and health departments for employees. It has become so commonplace that it seems fantastic that, as recently as thirty years ago, an employer pioneering in this direction had to place his plant hospital on a landscaped hill in plain sight of his workmen in order to allay dark fears of its purpose.

14

"To Rest Is to Rust"

In Armco's pioneering in industrial research, Carnahan was the original dynamo in the steelmaking end of the business. As he moved up in the organization, Beck understudied him. This was not difficult for Beck, who had learned under Westinghouse the value of continuous scientific inquiry in industrial practice.

But, as Beck later recalled, "As the company grew and the departments expanded, specialization became necessary and many perplexing problems came to us from customers."

Success was exacting its price. Mounting orders pre-empted first consideration and thrust aside that daring experimentation which, dominant in the early years, had made this plant "a research laboratory in the rough."

But new problems continued to come in; for, willy-nilly, the company was dedicated to specialization, and customers, old and new, always expected these specialists to know the answer to every question no matter how new or difficult it was.

In the early years most of the customers' inquiries filtered down through the organization to a pair of desks crowded in a wooden shack, no larger than a one-car garage, which had been the office of the construction engineers when the Curtis Street plant was being built. This shack was the headquarters of the open-hearth and rolling-mill superintendents. It housed also a cubbyhole "laboratory" of the company chemist.

Out of the unorganized palaver amid the chemical stinks in this shanty, a research department emerged as naturally as the grass grows.

In addition to this joke of a laboratory, there was an electrical "laboratory" in the motor-repair shop and electrical storeroom. By 1904 electrical research was cramped and a special building was erected to house its activities. By 1908 it demanded even larger quarters. A year later it was glaringly apparent that greater facilities would have to be created for both chemical and electrical tests and experiments.

At that point George Verity assembled a committee to ponder the problem.

"To rest is to rust," he said, unfolding his idea of a department whose function would be not merely the solution of customers' problems but a continuous search for new problems to be solved.

The upshot of the conference was the decision to combine chemical and electrical experiments and tests and house them in a specially designed three-story building. This new research building was erected across Curtis Street in Doty's Grove which the company had bought.

On September 22, 1910, Verity announced the creation of a research department with Beck as director. It was an innovation. The men in the mill humorously called it "Beck's brains bureau."

It incorporated a physical laboratory with apparatus for preparation of test samples. There was equipment for heat-treating research. There were facilities for chemical and microscopic investigation and testing of gas and fuel; a photographic section; a hall of exhibits, and offices for the research staff.

When the new department began to function in the following month, all operating department heads were informed of their relation to this novel clearing house for tough problems. Arrangements were made for exchange of information with the United States Bureau of Standards, Dr. Cushman's Institute of Industrial Research in Washington, the Westinghouse research department, and a number of research institutions in England and Germany.

Outside, proving grounds were laid out for testing materials subjected to the vagaries of weather. In a large field, hundreds of samples of the company's products were exposed to the elements and checked constantly. At another point, metal sheets were subjected to continuous water-spray tests and accurate records kept of their behavior.

These innovations were so bothersome and costly that questions often arose as to their worth, but Verity held out for their continuation, insisting that the policy would be valuable in the end.

Within a few years, the value of the innovation could be weighed. Other industrialists were coming here to study it and returning home to imitate it. By 1915, when the courts decided that the Carnahan patents 940,784-5, covering Ingot Iron, had been infringed, this research laboratory had become so famous that it was conducting many tests for other companies.

When visitors, having inspected this building filled with seekers and searchers, congratulated Verity on his foresight, he replied:

"Foresight? Not at all! Necessity mothered this invention. In the beginning, necessity decreed that each unit in our unique plan of operation be the smallest that could be built. Because our resources were so very limited, necessity dictated that we take our men into our confidence. Necessity then made us concentrate on quality, pushed us into electrical steel research and then compelled us to study the causes of corrosion. As our business increased, our intensive developmental research began to interfere with production of regular orders to such an extent that routine manufacturing processes were regularly upset; so, once again, necessity forced us to take the next step, a research laboratory.

"Our entire progress has been so accidental that it sometimes seems unreal to me."

15

Far Frontiers

IF ANYONE had suggested to George Verity in 1901 that his company would be doing business in South America in a little more than a decade, he would have considered the suggestion fantastic. Yet, at the very moment when he launched the little mill on Middletown's Curtis Street, the stage was being set, deep in a South American jungle, for exactly that "fantastic" accomplishment.

The particular act of his which was to make this jungle episode an important factor in his career was his decision, in 1907, that his company should advertise its new products in trade papers and engineering journals—a decision which he had to defend against those who deemed it a flagrant waste of money to advertise such a basic product as sheet steel, which was not often sold directly to the consumer.

At the turn of the century, the late Col. Hugh Lincoln Cooper, the hydraulic engineer who later achieved fame as the builder of Wilson Dam at Muscle Shoals and the mighty power project on the Dnieper River in the U.S.S.R., was directing an engineering program on a Brazilian jungle river.

One evening, just before night swooped down with that light-killing lunge characteristic of day's end in tropical jungles, the Spanish engineer operating the cableway over the river became impatient or careless and, yanking the wrong lever, dropped a scale box containing a crew of men into the churning waters below. Four men drowned almost instantly. A few escaped. Counting noses, Colonel Cooper asked anxiously:

"Where's Mario?"

Mario was a Brazilian boy, an exceptionally bright little fellow in whom Cooper had taken great interest. Scanning the rapids with his glasses, the Colonel looked sharply at a black speck beside a rock jutting midstream above the foaming water about five hundred feet down the rapids.

"It's Mario!" he shouted.

"In some way," Cooper later recalled, "the lad was able to get his legs and hands around the submerged boulder. All that could be seen was his head sticking out of the turbulent water."

Then the blackness of tropical night pounced on the jungle.

"We built a large bonfire on the shore nearest the boy," said Cooper, "and in its light we had an impromptu vaudeville show running all night to keep up Mario's courage so he would not lose his grip. About a hundred men took part in keeping the bonfire blazing high and having fist fights, wrestling matches, playing leapfrog, blind man's buff, and doing everything else we could think of to sustain a chap under such conditions. As soon as daylight permitted, we went out in a boat, fastened to a cableway, and slacked down among the rocks until Mario was reached and drawn into the boat, where, of course, the poor fellow immediately fainted away from sheer exhaustion.

"After a few hours he was quite himself again, and when I review the fine work he is doing for his native country, I thank the Almighty for the circumstances that intervened, permitting his useful life."

Long, indeed, was the arm of intervening circumstances on that occasion. That boy, Mario Y. Tebyrica, became Cooper's favorite pupil, learned English and engineering under him, became intensely interested in engineering developments in the United States and kept in touch with such developments through wide reading of U. S. technical journals.

In 1911 construction crews, toiling through the Brazilian interior, were building the difficult Pirus Pira Railway into the state of São Paulo. Their chief enemy was water, the implacable foe with which man contests eternally in the region of the Amazon—water, in its guises of torrential rain, land-soaking flood, breeder of fever-bearing mosquitoes, ally of lush vegetation and humidifier of hot air—water which, in one form or another, enables the jungle to erase quickly all trace of man's efforts to "tame nature" in the Brazilian forest. As the work progressed it became clear that erosion and corrosion would speedily undo it unless proper drainage could be devised. At that stage Dr. Tebyrica was summoned.

Thumbing through his latest batch of engineering journals from the United States, he saw an advertisement in which some astonishing claims of exceptional rust-resistance were made for culverts made of something called Armco Ingot Iron.

Impressed, he ordered a trial lot of culverts through one of those New York commission houses which were then the only channels open to South American buyers of United States products. Unfortunately for U. S. export business, most operators of such houses then practiced trade in the "good" old Yankee wooden-nutmeg tradition. Their trade theory was that South Americans were "Latin suckers" to be shaken down on the first order because there would be no second order—one of those tricky transpositions of cause and effect which too often constitute what "practical" businessmen call "common sense." Though the Yankee traders who got Tebyrica's order followed instructions specifying the Armco product, they tried to increase their profit by the neat little dodge of reducing the gauge specified.

When the order reached the Verity associates, they realized that the culverts requested were too light for the purpose mentioned. Since culverts of such thin gauge would not be fairly representative of the quality and service they advertised, they wrote directly to Dr. Tebyrica and ultimately sent him what he needed.

The result of this correspondence was the beginning of the company's globe-girdling export business, an activity subsequently carried on by its subsidiary, the Armco International Corporation.

This extension of the Verity influence to the far frontiers of the inhabited earth got under way shortly after the first correspondence with Dr. Tebyrica, when director Frank H. Simpson, brother of Verity's first partner in Armco, and Earl A. Emerson, a junior member of the sales force, made a trip to South America. After the two men circled the continent, Emerson was set up in the company's first overseas office, in Rio de Janeiro. Dr. Tebyrica came north to Middletown to study Armco policies and practices at close range. Returning to Brazil he secured a concession from the government to supply 80 per cent of the culverts used in the country, and he and Emerson set up Armco's first foreign fabricating plant.

Since unity is never achieved by talking about it, fine phrases alone will never allay the deep-seated Latin American distrust of the "Colossus of the North" and replace it with a "Good Neighbor policy."

Before the World War of 1914-18 few businessmen in the United States concerned themselves with the thought that good foreign relations and sound business practices might be two phases of the same fact. Fewer still cultivated such relations as patriotic duty. For, in those years, when the political foreign policy of the United States leaned dangerously toward that rapacious imperialism which, practiced freely by a few European nations, plunged those nations into war, the foreign policy of all too many United States businessmen bore a strong resemblance to the practices of confidence men.

Yet, even in that time, when our political heritage of "Manifest Destiny" and our high regard for the low trickeries of Yankee trading were giving the nation a sour reputation among "Yanqui"-distrusting Latins, the first seeds of good will and good neighborliness were being scattered in the southern Americas by George Verity's associates. Perhaps the unrolling scroll of history in the making will reveal this to be one of his best bequests to posterity.

16

A Club and a Catastrophe

BY 1911 the old house at 230 South Main Street had been transformed into a spacious and friendly place—a home that was being *lived* in. In the summer of that year it was as noisy and lively as a school dormitory, for Calvin, Leah and Sara, home from school, had each brought a number of their friends with them, and the Verity home resembled a young people's club.

Explaining the unusual activities in his home to his neighbors, George Verity said, "You see, Mrs. Verity and I were very young when our children came, and as they grew up, we tried to remain young with them in heart and mind. So we have made it our policy to have our children invite their friends into our home when and as they wish. We are happiest when every guest room is filled and the family table is surrounded by happy young people with healthy appetites. In a way, I suppose it is compensation for a great void in my own childhood and youth."

In his appraisal of the shortcomings of Middletown as a community he had stressed the fact that the town lacked facilities for wholesome recreation for youth. To provide it—at least partially—his own home and its surrounding grounds were converted into an unofficial club for the out-of-town friends of his children and the young folks who were their close associates in the community.

As these youngsters grew up, the Verity home became more and more a center of contact for an ever-expanding circle of friends and associates.

Host and hostess became "Uncle" and "Aunt," an indulgent couple with whom the girls and boys of this inner circle could share confidences more easily than they would with their own parents.

"We finally got to know so many of them so well, and loved them so much," he said, "that we thought of them as our own family and treated them as such."

As the summer of 1911 ended, "Dad" Verity, as he was now known to his children's friends, planned to create a club to knit the young people together. Preparing handsome leather-bound books, each containing photographs of every member of this accumulated family, a verse written for each one, and a charter of organization, he had the souvenirs delivered on Christmas morning of that year. With each book went a gold pin bearing the letters "D.V.C."

The original "Daddy Verity Club" contained only twelve girls and six boys, but the unusual family grew with the years. By the time the Veritys celebrated their fiftieth wedding anniversary, its growth had become such that an even fifty members came from their homes, from coast to coast, to help celebrate the event.

Outside his company and the ever-widening circle of his personal friends, acceptance of Verity's humane social and industrial ideas was slow. According to David Harlan, suspicion of his industrial reforms was quite general in the early years, and his proposals had to be patiently ingratiated into the community.

"I was the mouthpiece for many of them," said Harlan.

It was through Harlan that the Miami Valley Paper Manufacturers' Association was formed for the improvement of wages, hours and working conditions in the paper mills in the area. Next, again through Harlan, came a proposal that all local industries be organized for similar aims. Similarly, by easy steps, the Middletown Business Men's Club was transformed into a Chamber of Commerce, a planning board for the advancement of experiments in neighborliness, and that body became in due course the unique organization called the Middletown Civic Association.

Eventually the community's needs were met; its library and hospital were built; and its school system, expanded beyond the wildest dreams of the original planners, became one of the finest in the state.

But before these things were accomplished Middletown had to *become* a community. The catalyst for the transformation of factionalism into neighborliness was one of those terrifying demonstrations of power-on-a-rampage with which nature periodically reduces all men to the common level of helplessness.

"It took a flood to wash away our class prejudices," said Harlan.

The Great Miami River, lazily flowing just west of Middletown, is normally great in name only. During most of the year a tall man could wade across it at almost any point. In the springtime, however, it usually overflows its banks. But, in all the years within the memories of living men, its waters had seldom risen beyond the bottoms between the river proper and the city.

On the evening of March 24, 1913, some Middletonians began to worry about its sinister appearance. There had been an extremely cold winter with heavy snows, followed by a sudden March thaw and torrential rains. All that afternoon the racing river brought down parts of houses and barns. Along the bridge stood little groups of silent people with anxiety in their eyes and frightened children clinging to their hands. Throughout the night, reports came down from Piqua at the head of the valley that this was a super-flood. As a great wall of water swept down on Dayton, fear became panic.

Before dawn of the 25th, Bob Carnahan went to the bridgehead, took one look at the river, and scurried back into town to get men and women out of their beds and begin the organization of orderly evacuation and relief committees. By eight o'clock the canal was spilling its flood into the streets and its waters met the river's overflow surging up into the business district and the downtown residential area.

Having sounded the alarm and started the relief committees, Carnahan hastened to Armco's Curtis Street plant which, situated near the canal, was one of the city's principal danger points. All four furnaces were full of molten metal and any one of them was capable of generating a devastating steam explosion should water seep in.

The plant was virtually deserted, for, since early morning,

frantic women had been calling their men home to flooded houses. The few men who remained were working feverishly at the construction of a makeshift dam of steel, railroad ties, cinders and slag, trying to ward off the waves rolling down Curtis Street. One by one the little band was augmented by workmen returning after having moved their families into the hills east of town.

As each succeeding wave mounted higher than the previous one, they realized the hopelessness of their effort and left the dam, turning to the task of tapping the heat from the furnace most endangered. Just as the operation was completed, an enormous wave rolled down, flung the barrier aside and charged at the furnace. The fleeing men were rocked by an explosion as the water raced into the white-hot checker chambers and blew out all the sealed outlets. The roar and the immense column of steam added to the panic of the populace which was then either fleeing to the hills or trapped in upper stories of buildings.

Frantically now, the men threw barriers around the remaining furnaces, hoping and praying that the water could be kept away from the hot metal, and knowing that if it couldn't they would never live to tell the tale. Up and up and up came the flood—up to within six inches of the tapholes. The slag from the tapped furnace had been dumped into a ladle pit and the beleaguered men were horrified to discover that the water threatening to engulf them was actually boiling hot.

Then the waves loosened and upset oil tanks, and the oil seeped under the furnaces and caught fire. Now they were fighting two enemies. Bedeviled with the fear that the next second would be their last, they remained, working like demons, knowing that the feared explosion would destroy not only themselves but the whole neighborhood.

By nightfall, when the oil fires were extinguished and the worst dangers were lessened, the last of the men were ferried to safety on higher ground, leaving on rafts made of planks lashed to empty steel drums.

George Verity was in New York when news of the disaster was flashed across the country. The reports were meager, for the entire valley was cut off from the rest of the world by this flood which took 732 lives. All he could learn was that every community from Piqua to Hamilton was under water. One alarming report was that Middletown had been washed off the map. He caught a train—the first one available. It became the last one leaving New York for Cincinnati as the floods in the eastern tributaries of the Ohio River ended all contact between the Atlantic Seaboard and the Middle West.

Meantime his family and a group of neighbors were marooned in his home. With them were the family's three cows which Mrs. Verity had ordered brought into the house to save the animals from drowning.

For two days the refugees huddled on the second floor. On the third day, the water began to subside, but before dawn of that day panic struck again as men rowed through the streets shouting:

"Fly to the hills! Thirty feet more water coming down from Dayton!"

In the Verity home the warning struck terror into the hearts of the human occupants. First there was a frantic packing of bags and bedding in preparation for flight. Then Mrs. Verity, unable to wade through the deep and swift water in the street, decided to remain. All agreed to stay with her and they moved to the third floor, where they spent a night of horror in the darkness, wondering if they were high enough.

As dawn broke at last they peered into the half-light expecting to see the second floor engulfed. Instead, they discovered the flood was receding. Later they learned that the paralyzing warning of the previous day had been a false alarm.

That day the water level fell steadily. With it fell a deathly silence and a charnel-house stench.

George Verity was met on arrival in Cincinnati by one of his associates in an automobile and was assured of his family's safety. Loading the vehicle with every conceivable kind of supplies that might be needed by flood victims, he and his companion drove toward Middletown. The drive was a day-long ordeal of maneuvering over washed-out highways and slime-covered streets.

Arriving in Middletown almost five days after he had first heard of the disaster, he found his family safely housed with friends in the highlands east of the city, and then turned his attention to the community's needs.

Since the entire downtown area had been flooded, hundreds of people lacked shelter, dry clothing, food, drinking water and medical attention. Mud, filth and sewage lay ankle-deep upon the streets, sidewalks and the floors of homes and stores, menacing the health of survivors. The stench was nauseating. The water supply was polluted. An epidemic threatened. Marshaling his associates, mobilizing all Armco employees and turning out all the company's railroad dump-cars and construction equipment, he offered the full force of men and machines to the town in the drive to clean up the mess. The company brought in food, clothing and medical supplies, and lent its employees to help police the city against the looting that invariably follows disaster.

"Middletown became a community in the slime left by the flood," said Harlan. "We worked side by side, common laborer rubbing elbows with business executive. Men worked until they reeled with nausea. In that reeking mire we learned to understand one another. One morning, for instance, after we had been working all night, I noticed a man next to me who was violently ill. I told him to rest. In broken English he replied that he didn't want to shirk. He said he wished he could have some black coffee so that he could continue working. He hadn't been told that the women had set up canteens, so I took him to one of them where he was fed and ordered to rest.

"As we cleaned the streets, Armco rigged up pumping outfits, staffed them with crews and sent them from house to house, cleaning out basements and wells.

"After that awful ordeal the old frictions gradually gave way to understanding, and we began to think of ourselves as a more unified people."

The new spirit manifested itself immediately. As early as 1909 Verity and Harlan had been urging their fellow townsmen to build a city hospital. After the flood a school building had to be pressed into service as a shelter for the sick and injured, with local physicians volunteering their service. The makeshift served after a fashion, but the suffering was so acute and touched so many families that, when the proposal was revived after the flood, opposition had disappeared. Carnahan, who had endeared himself to the whole community by his work during and after the flood, became the dynamo for the drive which gave the town a real hospital.

After attending to the community's needs the Verity associates turned to their desolate Central Works on Curtis Street. Fortunately, the main operations had been moved to the new East Works which stood on high ground beyond the reach of the flood crest. "But Central Works," one of the veterans recalled, "was an appalling sight. The ruins, the silence and the odor reminded one of explorers' accounts of some Asiatic city abandoned because of pestilence."

After a complete cleaning and overhauling, the plant was again put into operation. Among the men who had worked heroically to save it from destruction were many to whom it had become "home." Flatly refusing jobs at the new East Works or anywhere else, they stayed on, some of them remaining and learning new tasks even after the old plant was converted into a foundry and fabricating unit.

The surrounding grounds were beautified with lawns and shrubbery, as were the banks of the adjoining Miami and Erie Canal. Eventually that abandoned waterway was filled in and converted into a boulevard which Middletonians named Verity Parkway.

Another aftermath of the flood was the adoption of the commission form of city government on August 8, 1913.

So complete was the reversal of attitude in this town that, in 1916, the citizens proposed George Verity as their nominee for Congress for their district. Declining their offer, he said:

"I feel I can serve best here."

17

Automotive Miracle

HAD the Verity associates gone ahead with their original plans to expand operations to the limits of the Curtis Street site, the flood might have ended the company's career. Their decision to build on a new site was—as subsequent events proved—the taking of the right step at the right time.

"It was again pure happen-so," said George Verity, "a step taken because circumstances demanded it. There was no long-range plan involved in it. Call it pure luck if you like."

In taking this important step he and his associates were, of course, looking beyond an immediate tomorrow toward probable needs for further expansion in the future; but it is inconceivable that any human mind could have charted a workable plan for the future in 1910. For, in that year, as many social historians have lately observed, there occurred a sharply defined change of tempo of life in the United States. The consequences of changes that emerged around that time are so enormous and so bafflingly interlocked as to be even at this date incalculable.

A century hence, historians may be able to say whether what happened in that time was a change in tempo or a change in direction in the march of civilization. Perhaps it was both. To try to interpret it would be clotted nonsense now. What, for instance, will be the ultimate social effects of wireless communication, with which thousands of boys were then playing? Of the replacement of the congestive steam engine by the dispersive electric motor, then taking place as power-transmission lines crawled across the land? Of such dispersive forces as the cinema, the airplane and the automobile, then rapidly evolving into practical, mile-minimizing agencies.

In the implementation of the power-transmission line the Verity associates had played no small part in the first five years of the century. And, in the second five years, they contributed much to the creation of the highways upon which the automobile was to run. In the third period, the automobile, changing rapidly from a hand-built luxury vehicle into mass-produced transport for the masses, repaid them handsomely for their pioneering.

When their new plant, sprawling over several hundred acres of farmland, was finished, the Verity associates were somewhat fearful that they might have overreached themselves. In one decade monthly production had climbed from 900 to 4,500 tons; the working organization from 350 to 1,500; the annual sales from $325,000 to $3,500,000. That was a ten-year growth, along with which the management had had time to grow. But now management faced not a growth but a leap—an overnight expansion surpassing in one bound all previous growth. They faced the monumental task of multiplying by three everything they had learned to do in their first ten years. To complicate matters, the rolls began to turn just as the nation's business dived into one of those storm cellars called "hard times" or "panic."

The full impact of that blow is recorded in the figures. In August, the first month of the new mill's operations, the output was 2,171 tons, considerably less than half the normal production before the plant was built. In the next month it fell to 172 tons, less than one-fifth the capacity of the original plant ten years earlier!

"All the elements of a terrific headache!" was the way George Verity described the dilemma. "Somehow we managed to survive, but it always seemed miraculous," he added.

The miraculous manifested itself in October, the third month, when tonnage crept back to 2,877 tons, near which figure it remained although business in general continued to decline.

The miracle involved was this: The automobile industry was beginning to come to Armco for sheets.

In the spring of 1911 the Verity associates had made their first auto-body sheets for Case and Kissel automobiles. Special grades of sheets they were, and tailored to customers' special requirements. To meet specifications, the sheets had to be cold-rolled on Saturdays when the hot mills were shut down and the men could give them special attention.

These sheets were used *on* rather than *in* automobiles, for carriage makers, thinking in terms of wood, were building motor-car bodies. After being fastened on the wood skeletons, the sheets were sandblasted and then given as many as twenty coats of paint. Between paint applications there were long periods for drying, to say nothing of long and laborious rubbings and putty glazings, all hand operations. About sixty days were needed to finish an automobile body. At that rate, this industry showed less promise of becoming a quantity user of steel than had the electrical industry of 1902. But, by this time, the Verity strategists had become adept at snapping up unconsidered trifles.

Such a trifle came to them about this time from a Detroit manufacturer of radiator shells. Sheets destined for radiator casings were subjected to such outlandish torture of twisting, drawing, folding and heating that ordinary steel could not stand it. The torture applied to steel for fenders was only slightly less severe. Most steelmakers tried to supply these things but eventually washed their hands of the business.

Here, obviously, was a problem for that gang of questioners in Beck's new laboratory. What do these automobile makers want? they asked. To get the answer they sent Chalmers Todd, the former office boy, to Detroit, Flint, Lansing, Pontiac and Toledo. Todd found that few of the motor-car makers themselves knew what they wanted. Steel was steel, as far as most of them were concerned. One after another, he learned, steelmakers had rushed in to take orders—and, one after another, had backed out as gracefully as possible before the onslaught of unreasonable demands.

"Better keep your hands off!" the veteran steel salesmen warned him. "All you'll get is burned fingers!"

But, back there in Middletown, there were idle mills and a research laboratory, and here was an industry with new sheet demands. Unreasonable demands? Well, there had been unreasonable demands before—demands which had turned out to be not so unreasonable after all.

So Todd assembled the problems of this industry and Beck's crew studied them. The new industry's needs were many. Special sheets for body panels. Another type for fenders and hoods. Another for radiator shells. Could Armco supply them? Well, Armco could try. And Todd set up a district office in Detroit with an affable salesman in charge to listen patiently to the unreasonable demands and transmit them to Middletown.

Just then the body builders decided to beautify the vehicles with curves. To get the curves, steel sheets were placed on leather-covered, shot-filled pads and pounded with wooden mauls. Ordinary steel stood that well enough. But then someone developed a machine to do the bumping and the manufacturers began heating the sheets to facilitate the process.

"Give us bumper quality!" was the new cry.

After the Verity strategists found out what was meant by "bumper quality," they tried to incorporate this new kind of toughness in their sheets. It was the nightmarish story of electrical steel and pure iron all over again. But out of it came something better than the automotive purchasing agents demanded, a steel with a silvery finish and an exceptional drawing quality. It answered to no specifications of that time. They called it Silver Finish auto steel, and informed the motor-car makers that it could be made in quantities sufficient for their needs. But when the price was mentioned, the automotive steel buyers howled, "You know what you can do with it!"

Before long, however, a few of them tried it, timidly. By 1913 it was estimated that this steel was being used in 50 per cent of Ford bodies alone, and some wag said, "Enough Armco

Silver Sheet has been sold in Detroit to put a roof over the town."

In June, 1912, Cadillac engineers ran into customer compaints about fenders. A delegation of the engineers toured the steel mills of the country, seeking a special kind of steel for fenders, but found no receptive ear until they reached Middletown and talked to Tytus.

"I think your demands can be met," said John.

Soon a carload of this special steel was finished. Because it had an exceptionally smooth surface, Cadillac accepted it and became a steady consumer. Other manufacturers, discovering that this more expensive steel's smoothness actually reduced the time and labor required to finish fenders, followed suit.

By 1913, the motor-car makers began yelling about "stretcher strains." To Todd the phrase was new, so he went to a factory from which a complaint had issued, and took with him Grant Broomall, Armco's chief inspector.

Recalling the incident, Todd said, "Broomall appeared puzzled at first when he was shown pieces of our steel broken by what were called stretcher strains. Then, after careful study and long deliberation, he removed his glasses and gently waved them at the complaining buyer's face, as he rendered in all seriousness this verdict:

" 'Well, what you people need is a sheet with a maximum of elongation but with a minimum amount of local reduction in area.' "

This double-talk, said Todd, apparently convinced the critic that Broomall had learned exactly what to do to correct the trouble, and everyone was satisfied—for a time.

But by 1914 the strains to which sheet steel was subjected in the manufacture of radiator shells brought another tough problem to the research department. Before it was solved, the Verity strategists had to develop new and revolutionary annealing furnaces and processes which altered some old practices in the sheet-steel industry and gave to the automobile industry a type of steel which would "flow" under the extreme pressures and twists applied by the deep-drawing presses.

Thus the new plant managed to keep its rolls turning and its furnaces roaring in the lean years of the pre-war depression. The automobile's growing demands were being met. The rolls in the mills were increasing—in number and speed. Electric motors were whirling them now. Elsewhere, electric motors were beginning to lift some of the huge burdens off the backs of men who rolled sheets. But the sheets were still being rolled in the same old way, and the dream of changing that way was becoming an annoying burr in the mind of John Tytus. He became assistant general superintendent of the Middletown division. He experimented as much as he could; but for a real experiment, millions of dollars would be required, and the millions were not available.

18

War

AFTER the flood the Veritys dug their expanded back yard out from under a layer of silt and filth, rebuilt their gardens and playground, and extended the boundaries by additional land purchase. Bit by bit they transformed the dismal chaos, falling away to the bottomlands, into a fine meadowland.

Then, in 1914, at the age of forty-eight, George Verity took his first vacation. Resting in a resort hotel in Georgia, he had his first introduction to golf. Returning, he laid out a one-hole practice "course" near the stable and tried to master the game.

Shortly afterward, a levee having been built along the river, he was offered an opportunity to purchase a thirty-acre tract of bottomlands, extending from Second to Sixth Streets. After he secured this property, mainly to prevent the reappearance of the shanty towns that were growing up along the river, he planned and laid out upon it a nine-hole course which later became the Verity Park Golf Club, a semi-public playground in the very heart of the city.

At work in the summer of that year he and his associates planned another innovation.

It was natural that such encouraging results as Dr. Tebyrica's response to the company's early advertisements should result in deeper study of the whole subject of advertising. It soon occurred to the strategists that, since the use of Ingot Iron was increasing steadily as base material in manufacture of household appliances, advertisements of its special qualities might be profitably directed to the individual consumer—the home-owner and the housewife.

This was a novel idea in its time—the second decade of this century, when advertising itself was only beginning to emerge, and the only products nationally advertised were such consumer goods as automobiles, ready-made clothing, breakfast foods, tobacco products, lotions, soaps, food and drink.

Great therefore was the consternation of steelmakers when the *Saturday Evening Post* for August 8, 1914, bore a double-page "spread" advertising Armco Ingot Iron, for this was the first time in history that a manufacturer of a basic material had chosen to speak directly to the ultimate consumer. Critics called it wasted effort, basing their opinion on the contention that the consumer, seeing only the finished product, knew little about the origin of the basic material, and cared less.

Though competitors scoffed, the Verity strategists continued the experiment, following with messages in *Collier's*, the *Literary Digest*, the *Scientific American*, the *World's Work*, *Outlook*, *System*, all the leading farm journals and trade magazines, and such newspapers as the *New York Times*, the *Cincinnati Enquirer*, the *Chicago Tribune*, the *San Francisco Examiner* and the *Pittsburgh Dispatch*.

Even advertising men doubted the efficacy of this program,

one of the first advertising campaigns launched on a nationwide scale in a comprehensive collection of of publications. But as the campaign progressed, the company's investigators found that consumers were asking salesmen about the kind of iron used in stoves and iceboxes. And, before long, manufacturers of such commodities, observing how they could capitalize on the company's campaign, included in their own advertisements claims that their products were made of Armco metals.

Later, virtually every steelmaker adopted the procedure, and it became common practice for basic-material manufacturers to "speak" to the hitherto ignored people who are the ultimate consumers of all products be they buttons or battleships, guns or butter.

In the month when this advertising campaign began, Europe's ultimate consumers were called upon to forget butter and consider guns. For it was 1914, and Europeans were once again concentrating on their favorite pastime—war.

The significance was plain to George Verity. Calling his employees together, he said:

"In Europe the peaceful occupations of cultivation and production have now been given up, and tremendous energies are being devoted to consumption and destruction. The accumulated wealth of many peoples will be largely destroyed. As far as material things go, they will have to start over again where they began many years ago. The material loss will be stupendous, but the loss in manpower will be appalling."

There was no satisfaction now in the thought that barbed

wire had been made more durable by the long and difficult contest with corrosion; for that product, designed for the peaceful, productive American farmer, was now being prostituted for subhuman ends between the trenches in Europe.

When the declaration of war stopped all American business in its tracks, Armco was weathering the pre-war depression better than most steel companies. In the first few months of 1915 a trickle of orders kept one turn working every day.

Then, suddenly, all hell broke loose as the first war orders piled in pell-mell. More speed! More speed! More orders, more shops, more buildings, more equipment. Everything was wanted *now.* Day and night more employees filed through the employment offices. Verity watched the flood of new hands engulfing the faithful stalwarts who had come this far with him, watched with sadness in his heart and a doubt about the organization's ability to absorb all these strangers into the pattern of co-operative square dealing he had been weaving so carefully.

For these war orders, the furnaces roared continuously, but the sheet mills lay idle.

The first order was for a million three-inch shells. It came on October 15, 1915. Hard on its heels came a request for one hundred thousand pounds of shrapnel shell forgings for Great Britain. Then another for the same amount. Then more and more and ever more. By June of 1916 a second expansion was started on a forge shop that had not existed a year before. Finally shells were forged under the open sky beside the great East Works.

April 17, 1917, came and the United States entered the war.

By the following November, American orders began to pile in, and times came when men lashed their weary bodies and minds into unbelievable tasks such as working sixty hours at a stretch. The selective service draft cut into the personnel. Key men among the strategists gave their services to the government. Then the influenza epidemic struck and twenty-four weary men died in one month from the forge-shop staff alone.

Came November 11, 1918, and the storm was gone with the suddenness with which it had come.

While the storm raged, Armco turned out 3,250,000 shell forgings, in addition to sheets for superstructures of submarine chasers, water jackets for Liberty motors, mines for the North Sea blockade, gun-carriages, and forgings for naval vessels.

Before the United States entered the war, the company sent to France a completely equipped ambulance corps, made up of volunteers from within the company. When the war ended, the men came back, loaded with honors from the French government. One of them, Newman Ebersole, subsequently married Sara Verity.

At war's end the Armco service flag bore nearly seven hundred stars, ten of them gold. In four Liberty Loan drives the employees in Middletown alone contributed more than $2,000,000. In addition they gave $74,000 to the Red Cross; and, voluntarily and upon the suggestion of Kristian Kronberg, an engineer in the plant, they created a special fund of $112,711 by self-taxation to help the families of Armco men in uniform and to rehabilitate the men when they returned.

Personally, George Verity sacrificed his favorite recreation by giving his beloved horses to the Army, and then plunged into the task of helping plan, build, equip and maintain recreation centers for men in training at Camp Sherman in Ohio.

During those years he also detected a weak spot in Armco's armor and set about correcting it. The company was now producing and processing steel from pig iron to finished product, but it was vulnerable because it was dependent on others for pig iron. Notified that the owners of the Columbus Iron and Steel Company, of Columbus, Ohio, were desirous of merging with a steel-producing company, he learned that this company not only owned blast furnaces, but controlled its own sources of ore, coal and limestone. A deal was therefore concluded in 1917 whereby Armco took over all the Columbus facilities—two blast furnaces, three coal mines, interests in a score of ore mines, almost ten thousand acres of timber, a fleet of nineteen Great Lakes ore carriers, a sinter plant, coke ovens and a long-term contract for limestone flux. With these additions, every step of the processes of steelmaking was now under control of the Armco management.

The pressure under which the Verity associates worked in these years is indicated by the tonnage figures. In 1915, output was 150,000 tons, the estimated full capacity of the company's units. In 1916 the lash of war demands upped output to 187,000 tons. In 1917 it became 219,000 tons. In 1918 it rose to 224,000. In the next year, as conditions fell back toward normal, it was 206,000 tons. But in 1920 it rose again, reaching the amazing total of 290,000 tons. All of which means that, in five years, with but slight increase of facilities, the output was nearly doubled.

Looking back over the first twenty years of his company's history, George Verity could count these gains:

A mill with a capacity of 900 tons a month had become a collection of plants capable of turning out 20,000 tons a month. Capitalization had increased from $500,000 to $34,200,000; annual sales, from $325,000 to $33,532,000; and an annual payroll of $196,000 shared by 350 had become one of $10,693,000 shared by 5,038.

The fourth five-year period was also marked by great losses. For on March 30, 1915, death took his good friend, William Simpson, after a long and painful illness.

Then, on January 30, 1917, the Reverend Jonathan Verity died, rich in years and honors.

Almost up to the moment of his death, the stalwart minister of the Gospel continued his work of "bringing souls into the Kingdom." In his seventies he toured the Holy Land, Europe and England, visited Pateley Bridge in Yorkshire and preached from the pulpit in which John Wesley had stood. Then, when he was seventy-eight, he went to the Orient to become a missionary in China and Japan.

The third great loss of the war years was the death of Robert Carnahan, the dynamic steelmaker whose fabulous exploits had become company legends even before he died in 1918.

At the Panama-Pacific International Exposition in San Francisco in 1915, Grand Prize certificates and medals were awarded to Carnahan, Moles and Armco for their achievement in the production of commercial iron of unprecedented purity.

"In the death of Carnahan," said George Verity, "we lost a great man."

19

Policy and Practice

"ONE of the big advantages of starting small and growing naturally is that we were thus able to weld our organization into something resembling a family," said George Verity to the visiting steel master.

This man, planning to build a steel mill near the Great Lakes, had asked:

"Why don't you move up into the Lakes region and get into the labor territory?"

"That," was the reply, "is exactly what we do not want to do. Here we are creating our own working and living conditions. Whether they succeed or fail, we alone are responsible for them. In one of those densely populous and highly industrialized areas which you speak of as a 'labor territory,' no one firm can shape its own destiny, for any one firm's backwardness or bad management can affect adversely the working and living conditions of every other group in that territory."

At the end of the fourth five-year period of his company's history, Verity had all the proof he needed that his humane policies, once called "visionary" and "impractical," constituted the best kind of business practice. In five terrible years of wartime turmoil, the men in his mills had doubled output with scant increase of operating equipment. During the great steel strike of 1919 the "labor territories" in which steel's major producers operated were scenes of violent unrest, savage strife, dark terrorism. While the storm raged, the Armco "family" went blithely about its collective business—making, rolling and fabricating steel.

Verity never pretended that his policies were philanthropic. On the contrary, he vehemently denied that they were anything more than plain common sense. He insisted that no enterprise can survive in the long run unless it is built on a solid foundation of complete honesty among management, men, capital and customer.

By 1919 he had demonstrated to his own satisfaction that, "once the foundation of honesty is laid, other benefits grow from it naturally, in their own good time, and such benefits accrue to all participants in the enterprise." His experience had proved that such things as decent wages and good working conditions, proper incentives to individual initiative and intelligent use of labor-saving equipment are potent forces which, spiraling outward into the whole community, and improving living conditions in constantly widening circles, finally come back to the place of their origin in the form of rich rewards to those who launched them.

It was natural, therefore, that his theories should evolve eventually into a specific "bill of rights." Tested in the fires of adversity, hammered on the anvils of experience, the policies he conceived in the formative years of the company were finally deemed so valuable that his associates urged him to put them into writing in 1919 and submit them to the board of directors for their approval. After serious study of the responsibilities and obligations which the company would have to assume through official adoption of such policies, the directors approved them as the platform upon which the company would henceforth stand.

Authorization and guarantee by a company of its management's policies, affecting not only employees and customers but also the communities in which it conducts its operations, was an unusual procedure. It turned out to be one of the most effective steps ever taken in the field of public relations.

Though published and approved twenty years ago, the document titled "Armco Policies" is still unique as a registered bill of rights for employees, a pledge of good faith to the community, and a guarantee of honesty to customers. Printed copies are available to anyone having dealings of any kind with the company.

In it, the company addressed the public thus:

"The American Rolling Mill Company was organized to provide a permanently profitable investment through the manufacture of special grades of iron and steel required in the fabrication of such products as might, from time to time, be demanded in an ever broadening field."

In effect, the Verity associates said, "We are in business primarily for profit," which is indeed a refreshing breath of candor amid the fog of phony altruism with which all too many enterprisers futilely attempt to becloud the obvious.

Next, the company says that, "to secure such a result in the largest measure, its organizers believed that it would be necessary to adopt and practice such policies as would bring about a condition of mutual confidence and create a spirit of sympathy and of real co-operation between the members of its working organization, its customers, its stockholders, and the citizens of the communities in which its plants would be located."

Then, in eleven plainly worded paragraphs, the policies are stated. That done, the document addresses itself more specifically to its management, its men and, finally, the community.

It is, in effect, a declaration of intentions by, and a constitution for, an industrial democracy. Its special significance to employees is that, though given to every new employee with an explanation that it embodies the company's rules, it is a code of ethics, rather than the usual collection of prohibitory "thou-shalt-nots." The "rules," one discovers, are nothing more nor less than the simple courtesies which free men must agree upon in order to remain men and free. Their "enforcement" is so automatic that many a manufacturer, having visited the company's plants, has gone away muttering his conviction that what he has witnessed—the manufacture of steel without the presence of stalwart armed plant police—must be a trick done with mirrors.

In this day and age, when lying has been raised to the condition of a fine art by the master craftsmen of propaganda and public relations, the mere words of this document are, of course, open to suspicion. Indeed, they are worthless—without the buttressing fabric of deeds.

Because they were thus bolstered when first placed before the employees, there was no occasion to doubt their value. For, when they were published, the company had embarked upon another innovation—the adoption of the three-shift day, a practice which many steel masters vehemently denounced as "utterly impractical" for several years after it was here introduced.

Not long ago it was custom in the steel industry for men to work at least twelve hours a day at their hot and heavy tasks. The seven-day work week was commonplace.

Time and again men struck against the custom, and their strikes, achieving nothing, became dark chapters in the history of steel. Clergymen denounced the practice and were branded "meddlesome preachers" by many of the heavy-handed lords of steel. Criticism by social-minded writers was called either "nonsense" or "radical agitation." Stubbornly, the "statesmen of steel" maintained that, since most steelmaking processes were continuous in nature, all talk about shortening the hours of labor was impractical—or worse.

The amazing thing about the persistence of the practice is that the use of three eight-hour shifts was not only tried but proved more efficient and profitable as long ago as the eighteen-seventies. The man who tried it was Carnegie's famous Captain Bill Jones, who reported its superior effectiveness in detail in a paper read before members of the British Iron and Steel Institute in 1881. His discovery was lost sight of in the smoke of the Homestead massacre, when many of the hard-won rights of the steel industry's labor were wiped out by an unfortunate strike.

Once more, in the nineties, there was an exception to the rule—an exception so superior in resultant output and profit that the steel masters' failure to gauge its significance is an amazing example of the ease with which the obvious may be overlooked.

Around the turn of the century, the Joliet Works of the Illinois Steel Company were famed for two things—the nation's fastest and most efficient rod-mill crews, and the eight-hour turn. So famous were this mill's craftsmen that special provisions had to be made to accommodate visitors who came by the hundreds to watch the men at work.

Somehow, the possibility of a relation between the two facts of the plant's uniqueness seems to have been overlooked by self-styled "statesmen of steel," for, after the Joliet mill changed owners during the years of the mergers, the story of its men's accomplishments was forgotten.

Forgotten? Well, perhaps not forgotten so much as ignored; for, in those teeming steelmaking centers in what Verity's visitor called "the labor territory," it was, as Verity pointed out, virtually impossible for any one firm to shape its own destiny because the backwardness or poor management of any other firm in the area was bound to have an adverse effect on working and living conditions in the territory.

In 1917-18 the exigencies of war underlined the importance of the men in the mills. They heard themselves called "soldiers in the second-line trenches"—men whose labor produced the guns, shells, tanks, destroyers, bayonets and barbed wire upon which victory depended. At the end of the war they believed it; and, in 1919, the steel workers struck. Their strike flared into violence throughout the so-called "labor territory," while production continued in peace in all the plants where the Verity associates worked.

The strike failed. Then the truth about its causes was forced into the open by a pair of reports which focused national attention on the twelve-hour turn and the seven-day week. One report, prepared for clergymen in the Interchurch World Movement, attacked the custom in its social aspects. The other, prepared in 1921, was based on a survey conducted by the Federated American Engineering Societies which reported that reduction of hours, wherever tried, had actually increased efficiency.

In June of 1923 the Federal Council of Churches joined the attack on the custom with its report, and President Warren G. Harding summoned the steel masters to Washington to discuss corrective methods.

Upshot of the White House conference was a public statement in which the steelmakers said the abolition of the twelve-hour day was desirable "if, and when, practicable."

It was a full decade before this White House conference—1913 to be exact—that the Verity associates began their studies of the eight-hour day with the hope of eliminating the twelve-hour turn on all continuous jobs. Perhaps their studies began because George Verity remembered those ninety-nine-hour weeks he had put in as a grocery manager. Perhaps the Verity associates began them because, being outside "the labor territory," they were less restricted by the strangling grip of custom. But, whatever the reason, they began their studies a full ten years before President Harding called the famous conference of steel masters.

Now, one of the objections which the old-line steel masters offered to the proposed change was that the workers themselves were opposed to shorter hours. Fantastic though it seems today, this was actually true—in the "labor territory," where workers feared the eight-hour day as a possible trick to reduce wages.

Superintendent Hook, who became the spearhead of the Verity associates' attempt to shorten the hours of labor, attributed the ultimate success largely to the fact that the experiment was an adventure in which management and men participated in complete confidence in each other.

"We approached the problem," he said, "from the standpoint of what was best in efficient operation of the company. We believed that safe and pleasant working conditions made for more efficient operations. So we began thinking of three shifts on twenty-four-hour operations long before we could apply what we had in mind to try."

When the time arrived for making a test, the proposal was placed before the men. The management reasoned that the change would give men more time for recreation and self-improvement; that it would make for a better community; that men would be healthier and therefore more efficient; that their improved efficiency should compensate for the cost of hiring additional labor for the third turn. A majority of the men, though expressing skepticism about the economic aspects, indicated their willingness to try the experiment.

The first trial was made in the galvanizing department, where men worked hard in acid fumes. The experiment was a success. The increased labor costs were more than offset by increased production per man-hour.

The preliminary findings of this experiment were turned

over to a committee for further study. This committee was headed by George Verity's son, Calvin, who had been familiarizing himself with labor's viewpoint since his boyhood days. From 1904 on, he had spent every school vacation at work—in the machine shop, the electrical repair shop, the open-hearth department, the electrical testing laboratory, with construction engineers and in an automobile factory. After graduation from Cornell University as a mechanical engineer, he had worked in the power-house pump room, as a foreman in the boilerhouse, as clerk in the motive-power division, and as construction foreman supervising the building of soaking pits, furnaces, picklers and a warehouse. In 1914 he worked in the sheet-mill department and conducted special studies of cold-roll operations.

By 1915 Calvin's understanding of labor's problems was deemed sufficient to enable him to take on, as assistant to the general superintendent, the study of operation costs with a view toward the change-over.

In 1916 the men in the blooming mill were called together and informed of the proposal to change to a three-turn day in their department. They responded effectively, and many of the suggestions adopted originated with the men on the jobs. Hook often recalled how a shear operator responded by suggesting a simple change in the placement of electrical controls which enabled two three-man crews on twelve-hour turns to become three two-man teams on eight-hour shifts.

"Though this particular change-over involved promotions of men to higher rates of pay," he said, "the resultant increase in output made up for the added cost."

By June of 1920, the three-shift plan was made official for all tasks involving continuous operations.

And the results? As previously noted, one result was doubled output with scant increase of facilities. In addition, unit costs of production fell though the per-day pay of men was raised. All this, mind you, in the wartime and post-war periods of rapidly rising costs!

The change-over was far from simple. It turned up many complex problems. It also turned up a few amusing incidents. John Tytus, for instance, found it hard to believe his ears when an emissary representing a group of foreign-born workers brought him their plea to be allowed to return to the twelve-hour schedule.

"Why?" he asked.

"They get ten cents a day less when they work only eight hours," said emissary.

"Ten cents!" John exclaimed. "Do you mean to tell me that men are willing to work four extra hours a day for ten cents?"

"Well," said the emissary, "ten cents is ten cents, and the men would rather have it than four hours."

Tytus refused to believe it. Investigating it himself, he uncovered the amazing fact that these men, mostly from southeastern Europe, preferred the longer hours for the extra ten cents because they had come to America to assemble a fixed sum of money and then return to their homelands to buy farms.

"They looked upon their stay in this country as a sort of prison sentence," he said; "hence that ten-cent loss was tragic because it extended the time they had to spend in exile. After we adjusted their pay scale, they were happy. Most of them, incidentally, remained and became good Americans."

Little by little, the steel industry came around to acceptance of the eight-hour day. Miss S. Adele Shaw, in an account of this pioneering by the Verity associates, published in the *New York Evening Post* of July 21, 1923, expressed it:

"The results of the three-shift experiment in the Armco mills are highly enlightening in view of the report opposing the elimination of the twelve-hour day made recently by a committee of steel leaders. But with the industry now apparently obligated to begin an intensive campaign for the change to the new system, the statement of Charles R. Hook, in which he shows the plan has been a success in the Armco plants, may prove to be one of the most important ever made in the controversy which for sixteen years has been before the public."

In 1934 Dr. Bradley Stoughton, the steel metallurgist who had directed the survey undertaken by the Federated American Engineering Societies, concluded that shorter hours undoubtedly contributed much to the unprecedented advance in technique and quality of production achieved by the industry after the appalling inefficiency of the twelve-hour shift was ended. It is extremely unlikely that the increasingly heavy demands for high-quality alloy steels—essential to the development of such modern tools as the automobile and the airplane—could have been met had the industry been able to cling longer to the old system; for, as George Verity and his associates demonstrated, the production of such specialty steels calls for keen, alert craftsmen.

"Only the freeman . . ." said Justus von Liebig, "has a disposition and interest to improve implements or to invent them; accordingly, in the devising of a complicated machine, the workmen employed upon it are generally co-inventors. . . . The improvement of established industrial methods by slaves, themselves industrial machines, is out of the question."

20

Middletown Raises a Million

WHAT the policies of George Verity accomplished in industrial relations, they wrought also in relations between industry and the community.

"A community," he said, "is helped best whose people help one another most."

Though the flood had broken down the barriers of suspicion in the community, improvement of civic conditions in accordance with his wishes did not gain real momentum until after the war.

After 1914, when the people of America were besieged with increasing pleas for help, the Middletown Chamber of Commerce organized a committee to raise relief funds with the least effort, conflict and expense. Ultimately there were two hundred and fifty men and women handling such collections. Representing all trades, industries and professions, drawn from all classes, creeds and nationalities, they operated so effectively that every quota was oversubscribed in record time, some collections bringing together more than four times the stipulated sums.

Then the war ended and the committee disbanded.

During the war and immediately afterward, the cost of

living rose rapidly, bringing great distress to people whose incomes were somewhat fixed. Especially hard hit were civic employees. As a result, Middletown's best schoolteachers, firemen, policemen and civic workers left to work elsewhere for higher wages, and community affairs drifted backward. At that point, Middletonians again asked George Verity if he had any suggestions. He proposed the application of what he called "intelligent selfishness."

"To be efficiently selfish," he said, "we must be generously unselfish."

Enumerating the community's accomplishments in the previous decade and itemizing the current needs, he pointed out that the flood and the war had provided the town with concrete evidence that its citizens could solve great problems through the use of that form of co-operative effort in which groups of individuals gain group rewards greater by far than the sum total of rewards attainable through individual striving.

"Middletown," he said, "raised over $6,650,000 in eighteen months during the war. Can we, in the face of that record, admit that we are not willing and able to provide for our own legitimate community needs?"

The talents of the people who had raised that sum for the nation and other countries, he said, should now be used to enable this community to help itself.

Everyone agreed it was a good idea. The committee was reassembled and a meeting was called to consider his proposal. As Harlan, who was chairman, recalled it:

"There was tremendous enthusiasm—until Verity proposed

that we raise a million dollars. A million dollars! In a community of thirty thousand people! Everyone was stunned.

"Then, after he had knocked the wind out of us, he pulled a piece of paper from his pocket and read his suggestion for raising the money. He said his formula was a tentative proposal. Based on the number of his company's employees, the value of its plant and the earnings of the past four years, it indicated, when compared with similar estimates of other Middletown industries, that his company and employees would have to 'tax' themselves for about sixty per cent of the total amount.

"When the rest of us applied the same formula to our own businesses, we saw how fair it was and decided the task would not be as difficult as it had seemed at first."

The collectors were called together, the details of the plan were worked out, and the collection began. In the final plan, the collection of subscriptions was distributed over a period of three years, and each industry agreed to work out its own formula of self-taxation and collection. In some companies employees pledged sums to be deducted from each pay check. In most cases employers pledged to match employees' contributions dollar for dollar. All funds were to be invested in government bonds as fast as received. Within thirty days after the plan was proposed, the million was pledged and payments began rolling in regularly from about nine thousand contributors.

That million-dollar campaign, widely publicized in the nation's press, was the beginning of modern Middletown. The city's hospital was enlarged. Funds were allocated to the board of education and the city government to raise the pay of teachers, policemen and firemen. A Y.M.C.A. was built. An old mansion was bought and converted into a war memorial and American Legion Home.

In a little more than a year, the fund balance (including unpaid pledges) was $1,028,303.87. At first, administration and distribution were in the hands of the Chamber of Commerce. On August 29, 1923, that body disbanded itself because its name did not fit its broadened activities, and the Middletown Civic Association, incorporated a month later, succeeded it.

This Association is unique. In a sense, it is a continuing Community Chest. However, it is also a semi-governmental agency since it shoulders tasks ordinarily borne by tax-maintained municipal agencies. Moreover, it handles all of the community's relief problems, thus divorcing relief from politics. City and state welfare funds are allocated to it for distribution. Since it bears the cost of administration, all such relief funds are used for relief. It has never encountered that situation experienced by so many Ohio towns—the depletion of welfare funds in mid-year.

It operates a summer camp for underprivileged children. It maintains a camp for the exclusive use of Boy Scouts on a 133-acre tract deeded to it by Charles R. Hook.

An interesting item in its history is the record of a gift of $85,000 from Armco employees. This sum was the undistributed residue of the employees' wartime contributions to their private fund for the aid of families of men serving in the armed forces. After the war, Armco's Middletown, Zanesville and Columbus employees found themselves in possession of funds for which there were no further demands. Columbus employees voted to turn their money over to their branch of the Armco Association for its relief projects. The Zanesville portion was used to build a fine memorial athletic park opposite the plant entrance in that city. In Middletown the employees voted almost unanimously to turn their portion over to the community through the Civic Association.

Today this unique organization is maintained on an annual budget of about $100,000. Its funds are raised by a small staff of collectors from individual donors. The largest portion comes from industry, in which each company has its own rules of self-taxation. In many companies, when a man is hired he agrees to contribute a small portion of his earnings to the fund. His contribution may be a portion of his weekly pay or an hour or so out of each month; but, whatever the arrangement, his employer more than matches his contribution. Thus, in all Middletown, there is scarcely an employer or employee who is not voluntarily taxing himself to help his community.

The Association operates from a rebuilt old mansion containing two public meeting rooms and an auditorium, all available for public meetings of nonsectarian and nonpartisan nature. It houses and maintains the town's Red Cross chapter, and a Bureau of Public Health which conducts four clinics. Its Bureau of Commerce handles tasks usually taken care of by chambers of commerce. Its Family Service Bureau handles relief problems and dispenses welfare funds and surplus commodities. It co-ordinates the activities of Boy Scouts and Girl Scouts, handles the problems of war veterans, and allocates funds to Garfield Mission, the Salvation Army, the Middletown Hospital and the Y.M.C.A.

It is a community's expression of the realization that co-operation is not a sentiment but a necessity. It is a Verity dream realized.

Tapping the heat! The most spectacular scene of steel is when the liquid metal is run out of the open-hearth furnace into a giant ladle.

Pouring the steel from the ladle into ingot molds with the aid of a huge traveling overhead crane.

21

John Tackles His Job

By 1920 the time had come for another dream to be realized.

After John Tytus had proved his ability by almost four years of successful management of the sheet mill at Zanesville, he was summoned back to Middletown at the end of 1909 to supervise the installation and operation of the large collection of manual-type sheet mills at East Works. Thus brought close together again, he and Hook resumed discussions of their hope of improving sheet-rolling methods.

By 1910 the stage was being set for such improvements; for in that year the electric power transmission lines, vastly extended through the use of greatly improved transformers, began to feed energy into the first motors in steel mills. Though the significance of this technological innovation was not apparent then, a retrospective appraisal throws a bright light on its relation to a job which Tytus was being prepared to tackle.

Just after Tytus had installed the manual mills which he was growing to dislike mightily, there had come that strange lull during which the mills were kept going only because the builders of automobiles wanted special grades of sheet steel.

On July 1, 1913, he was again made assistant to Charlie

Hook, who had now become general superintendent of all the company's plants.

The war began, and while furnaces roared and forging equipment had to be installed under the open sky to meet war demands, the sheet mills were virtually idle.

The Hook-Tytus discussions continued. One of them brought up questions of sheet-mill practice of such radical nature that Hook took Tytus to Columbus, Ohio, to confer with Vice President Joseph H. Frantz, who was in charge of the company's recently acquired blast furnaces. Frantz had many years of experience in the practices of rolling sheets and, though a very practical man, possessed an analytical mind which was not closed to novel ideas.

As a result of this conference, some bold experiments were undertaken in an attempt to improve methods of rolling sheets of heavy gauges, which proved to be of great value later on.

Tytus played with those almost idle mills, arranging them this way and that way, converting them into a fantastic laboratory for trials of his mind-irritating idea. Here again he learned, through fingers and muscles, the things that books couldn't tell him.

The war had shut off foreign labor. The mill's demands for hands were met by brawny men from Kentucky. "Not so good as hunkies," some labor bosses said of them. "Too independent!" John disagreed. He liked these independent Americans. Inheritors of the American tinkering tradition and capable of using their heads as well as their hands, they were willing to lend a hand on a job even when the job looked ridiculous.

"You can't beat them for intelligence," he said. And they tinkered together, trying to make machines do what they were not designed to do—trying and failing, smashing equipment and laughing about it, and trying again.

Now it was 1920, and he and the "boys" had played with rearrangements of mills until he was positive they could do what the experts said was impossible. His dream had now grown into a great roll of sketches and charts. He and Charlie Hook were studying them often now—studying them and thinking it was about time for this "crazy" idea to get itself born.

Yes, though neither Hook nor Tytus realized it, the time was fast arriving for those lines on the sketches and charts to be translated into lines of steel rolls and chains and motors. The need had begun to emerge back there in 1912 when the rolls were lazily turning out special sheets for Detroit, Toledo, Flint and Pontiac. For in that year (1912) the shops into which those sheets were going were discovered by Wall Street, and, overnight, "the automobile game" became "the automobile industry."

As Wall Street listed the first motor-car stocks and thus accorded recognition to a new industry, there were signs and portents that it might become a great industry. The Selden patent suit was settled that year; and the "tin Lizzies" rolled off the Ford assembly lines. Henry M. Leland incorporated in his 1912 Cadillacs the amazing electric starters of Charles Franklin Kettering, ending the monopoly of the driver's seat long held by men with strong right arms. And Edward Gowen Budd of Philadelphia proposed his "heresy"—the all-steel body, which, scorned by the industry's ex-carriage-makers as "ridiculous" and "cheap," attracted the attention of General Motors' president, Charles W. Nash, and, a little later, John and Horace Dodge.

There was a ray of hope for Tytus and Hook when the war ended. The huge forge shop, built for forging shells, was useless now that nobody wanted munitions. Looking at that idle shop and the increased open-hearth capacity, the Verity associates asked, "What shall we do with all the steel we are now able to make?"

For they could make it, but not roll it. Should they sell the surplus? Should they add rolling equipment? Should they toss the wartime forge shop on the scrap pile?

To ponder these questions a committee was born. Out of the committee's deliberations came the suggestion that this might be the heaven-sent opportunity to give the Tytus dream a whirl. Not a bad idea, George Verity and Charlie Hook agreed. But would the directors agree? They would.

The order was given to install an experimental continuous mill unit for the rolling of the heavier gauges demanded by the trade.

Go ahead, John!

But before he could get his sketches unrolled, the sales department was suddenly snowed under by a blizzard of orders. Demand for sheets of lighter gauges became so pressing that the Verity associates reluctantly decided to give up the idea of an experimental mill and install four new standard mills at Zanesville instead.

Americans were now buying new kitchen stoves, washing machines, refrigerators, automobiles, all manner of new things—steel things. Not only Americans, but all the civilized world. There were orders from the company's reopening outlets in Europe. There were orders from the outposts in South America, Asia and the Pacific islands which the company's export department had developed during the war. From outposts in Johannesburg, Durban, Cape Town and Port Elizabeth came orders for the specialty steels whose blue-triangle trade-mark was now becoming famous even in Africa. Returning from the Orient, secretary Phillips brought orders for culverts and flumes from Java, India, China, Japan and the Philippines. And into Australia that year, Armco shipped more sheet steel than all other American steelmakers combined.

So Tytus rolled up his blueprints, sighed, and set to work installing more of the manual mills which he was determined he would one day render as obsolete as oxcarts and antimacassars.

While Tytus labored with his faithful "boys," there came to Verity's desk an attractive offer of properties and plants of the Ashland Iron and Mining Company in Ashland, Kentucky. The price was ridiculously low for this property planted right in the heart of the coal beds where Kentucky, Ohio and West Virginia meet. There were two blast furnaces, six open-hearth furnaces, a blooming mill, coal deposits, but virtually no finishing department.

Now, the Verity associates had been contemplating increasing blast-furnace capacity at Middletown because the Columbus furnaces were inadequate and too far from the company's plants and raw-material supplies. The Ashland offer was therefore attractive, not only because of the blast furnaces, but also because the properties embraced some twenty thousand acres of coal, timber and natural gas lands, and interests in a coal-carrying railroad.

But no finishing department! Of what use would it be to Armco, which was right now trying to bring its own finishing facilities into step with its expanded steelmaking capacity? No, thank you, said George Verity.

This happened as 1920's calendars were tossed into wastebaskets. Then came the post-war depression. For two years the demands for sheet steel had been insatiable as Armco's personnel increased from 3,850 to 5,845. Then, suddenly, nobody wanted the stuff, and the price fell from $110 a ton to $50, plunging $25 in six weeks. Armco's personnel dropped back to 3,868 in a year.

Now an even more attractive offer came from Ashland. Studying it, the Verity associates saw that this half-a-plant was a natural setting for the postponed experiment.

As 1921's calendars in their turn were discarded the properties were bought.

Go ahead, John!

And Tytus grabbed his blueprints and went away from there as fast as possible for fear he'd be stopped in his tracks again. First he built a high fence around that part of the Ashland plant which was to be his laboratory. Rumors had spread through the industry that he was playing with an idea that had been proved impractical again and again, but steel masters who heard them remembered earlier rumors of "crazy" ideas in Middletown which had rattled the back teeth of scoffers by becoming accomplishments.

So John built his fence high and stout, brought about a hundred faithful, close-mouthed co-inventors over from Middletown, moved into the mill with them, and locked and guarded the gates as if this were Kentucky of yesteryear with Indians on the prowl.

Inside, he and the "boys" set to work. They worked until they were ready to drop with weariness; and when they were ready to drop, they dropped and slept where they dropped. When their nerves became so tight that they threatened to slam fists in friends' faces, tensions were released with cards, poker chips, bottles and glasses.

Into the wastebasket went 1922. Into the experiment went millions.

"The biggest job," said Tytus later, "was to get up the nerve to recommend the enormous expenditure required to test the idea. The best-informed men in the industry had by now conceded that what we were trying to do was possible—if one had the nerve and the money. Without the assurance of Mr. Verity's faith in the idea, I don't think I would have had the nerve to tackle the experiment or continue it."

Continue it they did; and into the wastebasket went 1923.

On the very last day of that year, the first unit—the heavy sheet mill—was complete. But would it work?

If this were fiction it would be nice to say that John Tytus pressed a button and a four-ton, white-hot ingot slid from a furnace through a succession of rolls and shears that squeezed and cut it into a smoothly flowing river of broad, thin, cherry-red steel, for that is how the process works nowadays.

But this is not fiction, and it must be said that it worked—after a fashion. Rolls broke. Housings snapped. Sheets buckled. The device was as full of "bugs" as a lumber-camp bunkhouse.

By January of 1924 the installation was complete—a bar-plate mill of seven stands (individual mills), a roughing sheet mill of seven stands, and finishing sheet mill of five stands.

Theoretically, this succession of mills, all linked together with what might be called "moving assembly lines," should have flipped out sheets of steel somewhat as John and his poker-playing associates dealt cards. It did, but not quite so easily.

For one thing, there was an awful mess of those buckled sheets called "cobbles." There were so many of them that one veteran roller actually wept. He had been rolling for years and had become such a proud craftsman that he considered it a blot on his reputation if he had to discard more than two cobbles in a turn. So, when he had to stand helplessly beside these mills and see more cobbles in a day than a decent roller should see in a year, it was a knife in his heart, and he wept.

Tytus recalled that it was a long time before he was able to convince the man that the important thing was the ratio of good sheets to cobbles.

"It was largely due to the young men that the experiment progressed as it did," he added.

His "boys" were an ingenious lot. When something im-

Protected by shatter-proof glass, operators in pulpit (*upper left*) of the slab mill send an ingot rumbling between the rolls and reduce it to a slab, at the East Works Division, Middletown, Ohio.

A visual pyrometer is used to check the temperature of the steel as it races through the continuous hot-strip mill, East Works Division, Middletown.

portant broke, they could use baling wire or log chain with marvelous results. Once when they smashed an important part of the mechanism and there was neither time nor money to spare for a replacement, they worked out a "haywire" substitute, a device so weak that they had to operate in a new way. Thus they accidentally corrected a condition that had been threatening to throw the whole experiment into a tailspin of failure.

Armco's first problem was to perfect the mill mechanically. At the end of six months the management was satisfied on that score. The second problem was to get the mill to produce the 18,000 tons a month which engineers estimated it would have to turn out to justify itself. By the end of the first month of full operation it was rolling 350 tons a day, or about 9,000 tons a month.

That was only half enough. Into the experiment went more thought, more labor, more money, more weeks, months, years.

At the end of three years the mill was rolling about 40,000 tons a month.

In all the years it took to develop this new kind of mill, nobody could predict what the quality of its product would be. Would wide sheets, rolled in this new way, be worthless? The only way to learn about the quality was to try out the idea.

Unexpected was the discovery that the kneading effect of the process imparted to the metal qualities of surface and workability far superior to any ever attained on the old hand mills.

"So," said George Verity, "at the end of all these years, we knew where we stood. We had risked the whole future of our company on this experiment. Now we knew we would be repaid for the pioneering. Cost of production was substantially reduced. Volume was double the original estimate. Quality was better than we had ever deemed possible.

"In the years of development, we gave serious study to the possibility of patenting all phases of the revolutionary process. As the work progressed and it became plain that we had something extremely valuable, other steelmakers went to work on similar plans of their own. Eventually we had to decide whether we should try to keep control over the processes and hold a monopoly, or work with our competitors by sharing the benefits. We decided the co-operative way would be best in the long run. So we took all the principal steelmakers into our confidence, showed them what we had done, explained how basic the development was, let them see how it had affected volume and costs, and suggested the economic effects it could be calculated to produce. Then we explained the liberal terms under which we would grant licenses covering the use of a group of patents which had been developed."

Naturally, there were attempts at piracy, one of which resulted in court action. But, in the main, steelmakers deemed the Armco terms fair. Within a decade after the Ashland mill rolled its first sheets, an estimated half-a-billion dollars had been invested in twenty-seven continuous wide-strip mills in the United States, with a combined annual capacity of 14,000,000 tons.

Called "the most marvelous advance in steelmaking technology in our time," it shook the whole industry to its foundations. For years the giants of the industry had maintained their dominant positions with huge but obsolescent plants geared to tonnage production of "big stuff" for railroads, ships, armaments and the construction industry. To these giants, sheets were "small potatoes." On such "small potatoes"—sheets, specialties, alloy steels and the like—a group of small steelmakers, called "the independents," had grown up.

Then along came this revolutionary process for rolling sheets—at the very moment when the need for it was becoming urgent. Hard on its heels came the depression of 1929, bringing the collapse of construction and the end of the railroads' purchases of rails and rolling stock, and catching the giants flat-footed and off guard.

Now an amazing thing happened. While the great mills for the production of "big stuff" were tenanted only by spiders and could have returned to rust without having been missed by the public, the shops of Mesta, United Engineering and Foundry, Westinghouse and Mackintosh-Hemphill were roaring day and night, turning out millions of dollars' worth of continuous wide-strip mills for the steel plants of "the independents" in Detroit, Chicago, Cleveland and a half-dozen smaller towns in the Middle West. Almost overnight, "small potatoes" had become "big stuff," as public demand for thin-rolled steel steadily increased.

Why?

Part of the answer lies in a comparison of the following sets of facts:

In 1919 Americans bought 1,591,000 automobiles, paid an

average of $875 each for them. Ninety per cent of the vehicles were *open* cars.

In 1929 Americans bought 4,140,000 automobiles, paid an average of $630 each for them. Ninety per cent of the vehicles were *closed* cars.

In that decade the wood-and-iron horseless carriage was accelerating its evolution into the all-steel automobile.

All steel? A better term would be "all steels." For, in this evolution, steel had to become steels—specialty sheets, in whose perfection the Verity associates pioneered, and high-quality alloys which could not have been produced by brain-fagged and toil-worn "slaves of steel" under the old system of the twelve-hour turn and the seven-day week.

For such steels—the scorned "small potatoes" with which the small producers had had to be satisfied—the public demand was becoming insatiable by 1929. These steels were needed not only for automobiles, but for refrigerators, washing machines, ironers, filing cabinets, office machinery, furniture, kitchen and bathroom equipment, and a thousand and one other things. And, because they were small and nimble, "the independents" were quick to seize the Tytus invention and thrust sheets upon the throne of steel long preempted by rails.

Even the buyers of automobile sheets were incredulous—at first. For years their increasing clamors for "More sheets! More sheets!" had kept the old-style manual mills clattering and banging at capacity production as the mills' human attendants worked to the limits of endurance in frantic attempts to supply the demands. In the long line of operations between the ore deposits and the consumers of sheet steel, this was the bottleneck. Uncounted millions had been spent in futile attempts to widen it and permit a smooth flow from producer to consumer. Then, after the impossible had been achieved, it was hard to believe it had been done. Skeptics had to be convinced. The way in which they were convinced was not infrequently the hard way.

There was such an instance which Tytus always recalled with amusement.

An automobile-factory buyer, who derived considerable pleasure from his job of driving the salesmen of his steel supplier, was informed that the bottleneck had been cleared. His next order came through as usual, marked "Immediate delivery—*rush!*" It was an order for 800 tons of frame stock. The salesman called on him and asked:

"Do you mean immediate delivery?"

"Certainly, I mean it!" was the dictatorial reply.

"May I use your telephone to notify our mill?" the salesman asked.

The buyer waved toward the instrument. The connections completed, the salesman asked the mill manager if he could deliver the order immediately and, receiving assurance that delivery would be made, requested the buyer to confirm the order personally, then and there.

That done, the new mill began to roll—at the rate of a hundred tons an hour. A day and a half later the complete order was on the automobile plant's railroad siding.

"It took them three weeks to unload the cars," Tytus said.

"After they paid the demurrage charges on the freight cars, they were convinced."

Today it is no longer marvelous that steel should be rolled in continuous strips, up to widths of 91 inches, with scarcely a man visible beside the roll trains that carry the roaring, hissing, red ribbons along at speeds up to twenty-four miles an hour. No, it is no longer marvelous—if the beholder's soul is dead. But it is so fascinating that the sight of it being done holds you spellbound, even after you have seen it dozens of times. For one thing, it involves the use of a machine too huge to be seen in one glance. It surpasses the descriptive power of ordinary folk. It must be seen to be believed. And when it is seen, it is still hard to believe that this mammoth machine is the product of the mind of man. Watching it work as smoothly as a river rolls, you steal sidelong glances toward the rafters, trying to catch a fleeting glimpse of the gods who manipulate it. And you are flabbergasted when you see that the "gods" are mere men, sitting comfortably in glass-walled, air-conditioned cabins suspended from the rafters—mere men, pressing electric control buttons, twirling little wheels and knobs, watching quivering needles of sensitive electric indicators record the speed and temperature and dimensions of the red river racing through the rolls.

You stand behind one of these men among the rafters and you hear him say, to nobody in particular, that the temperature of that last quarter-mile of steel was a little low. As you wonder if the remark was intended for your ears, you hear the reply come back from nowhere. This, you are told, was a conversation via radio between this operator and another one, a half-mile away, at the place where these rippling ribbons emerge from the soaking pits in the form of white-hot ingots as big as a telephone booth.

But it is useless to try to describe the thing. You ask an engineer to help you and he says, "The principle involved in the process can be stated in two words: progressive convexity."

"And that means what?" you ask.

The rolls between which the steel is passed, he tells you, are ground with an invisible concavity which induces the steel molecules to run straight through the stands, the edges of the sheet moving forward at the same rate of speed as the center.

Stand by stand, through rolls with progressively diminished concavity, the lengthening sheet's convexity is ironed out in accordance with the cooling metal's ability to tolerate the progressive squeezes.

"Oh!" you say, as if you understood it perfectly—which he knows you don't when you ask:

"Since the sheet is continuously growing longer, why doesn't it buckle between the stands of rolls?"

And, walking alongside the roaring monster with you, he cups his hands to his ear and yells the explanation that the electric-motor-driven rolls of each succeeding stand are revolving slightly faster than those of its predecessor.

At the last pass through the rolls, the metal, which began as an 18,000-pound ingot a mile away and a few minutes ago, has become a straight, thin, flat sheet clattering like a subway express train over a "table" (hundreds of whirling cylinders) toward a coiler whose poised steel claw pounces, seizes the forward end of the speeding ribbon of steel and coils it up like a spool of newsprint paper.

At that point you remember what you have heard about a time in 1904 when a young man, vaguely dissatisfied with his prospective future in a paper mill, astonished George Verity by asking for a chance to do the hard and heavy work which this amazing machine has now banished.

And you cannot help wondering if this great contribution to the metalworking arts would have been possible if George Verity had not pinned his faith to such men.

There were, of course, other contributions to the process after Armco pointed the way. Just after George Verity invited competing steelmakers to examine the Ashland mill in 1927, he learned that two young engineers, H. M. Naugle and A. J. Townsend, were hard at work on this old problem in a steel plant in Butler, Pennsylvania. Unlike Tytus, who had built the Ashland mills to roll short sheets which followed one another through the succession of stands, these men were attempting to roll wide strip, or sheets several hundred feet long.

Since the Armco patents covered processes for rolling material twenty or more inches wide, the Verity associates notified the Butler experimenters that they were probably infringing on Armco patents. The Butler people, who had obtained some patents of their own, studied the Tytus process and finally decided to sell their plants and patents to Armco.

The Butler purchase included a wheel company with a capacity of ten thousand tons of forged-steel railway-car wheels per month, and an old narrow-strip mill in Elyria, Ohio. The acquisition increased Armco's capacity to about a million tons of finished products a year, and its employees to ten thousand. The operations at Elyria were discontinued and the Butler plant was reorganized. It needed reorganization badly. Visiting it for the first time, Charlie Hook is said to have reacted like a man who has just seen a living dinosaur, when he learned that operations were conducted without a safety program.

"It took us most of the next two years to key this plant into our organization," said Hook.

To the Verity associates the purchase brought the problem of combining the best features of the partially developed process with the outstanding features of the Ashland mill. Months of refinement and improvement followed. Thus, many minds contributed to this revolutionary development.

After quiet, patient, soft-speaking John Tytus became a vice-president of Armco, a tiny, silver-plated rolling mill was placed on his desk by the men from whose backs he had lifted burdens which no human backs should have been expected to bear in the first place. Proud of the little token, he used it as a paperweight, valuing it more highly than the Gary Medal he was awarded in 1935 or the Modern Pioneers Award bestowed on him in 1939.

When men calling themselves "sociologists" spoke of the continuous wide-strip rolling mill as "a monster, because it throws men out of work," he would pick up this little silver mill and ask, quietly and politely:

"Did you ever try your hand at the kind of work it ended?"

True, the new process created great changes in employment. Doubtless there were steel plants in which veteran rollers were ruthlessly cast adrift. In the plants directed by George Verity, however, the revolution was humanized as much as possible by absorbing the displaced men in other jobs and paying them special separation allowances for six months to finance them through their readjustment.

Although the process displaced many men, it created an incalculable number of new jobs, in the steel industry and in all industries in which sheet steel is used. Within the steel mills, the new product called for many new processing operations. By halving the cost of sheet steel, the process created an enormous increase in use of its product. In every mill that employed the process, the first decade of its use brought marked increases in the number of workers and in the scale of wages.

In the final balancing of debits and credits it will probably prove to have been more ominous to capital than labor; for the cost of the machinery runs into so many millions that it is prohibitive to let the machinery loaf. At least one such machine has demonstrated its ability to produce four thousand tons in a single day. Thus the machine is easily able to race into costly idleness. This is capital's dilemma: Shall I share the machine's benefits with labor in the form of higher wages, and with the consumer in lower costs, and thus keep the machine rolling and bringing in a reasonable return of profit, or shall I take what the traffic will bear and race the process into a condition of idleness that is suicidal?

It is as yet too early to evaluate the social and economic effects. At the moment of this writing, America's capacity to roll sheets has expanded far beyond the capacity to produce ingots. To widen this new bottleneck engineers recently turned once more to the long unused Bessemer converters which, though requiring liquid charges and utilizing little scrap, can make steel in one-tenth the time required by the open-hearth furnaces. Applying techniques that were unknown when the converters were supplanted, the engineers are now modernizing them with flame-control equipment incorporating the photoelectric cell.

The destinies of nations are being shaped by the new process. Germany, Russia and Japan were among the first Eastern Hemisphere nations to sense its significance—and with what results?

In England its adoption by one company and the resultant fears of monopolists depending on outmoded processes produced repercussions in Threadneedle Street, played a part in the departure of the late Neville Chamberlain from Downing Street, and may be exerting considerable force upon history in the making at this moment.

It is currently playing an important role in the recent and phenomenal emergence of Australia as an industrial nation. In 1939, the Verity associates co-operated with John Lysaght, Ltd., long-established British steelmakers, in the construction and operation of the Commonwealth Rolling Mills plant at Port Kembla. Using the Armco-developed process, the Port Kembla mill became the first producer of high quality sheets south of the equator and the nucleus of the world's newest and fastest-growing steel-producing center.

Far-reaching, indeed, have been the effects of the collection of inventions which Armco introduced. When all the facts can be collected, it may turn out that George Verity and his boards of strategy fulminated more practical social explosions than all the social reformers of our time.

22

Harvest Years

WITHOUT a store of force to set it working, even a good idea cannot become an invention. Brooks Adams held that such stores of force "must always take the shape of money." But, since he added that the money must be in motion and not hoarded, he might as well have said that the leavening element is human faith, for hoarded money is frightened money and money in motion is faithful money.

As John Tytus himself has said, the great invention with which Armco revolutionized the steel industry could not have become a reality without the aid of George Verity's faith.

For that faith the Verity associates were well rewarded. The company prospered. To Verity himself the prosperity brought a red-letter day in 1928.

"In that year," he said, "I sold some of my Armco shares and got out of debt for the first time in over thirty years. After that, I lived and worked within my income. I had to!"

In comparison with most steel executives' remuneration as revealed by the Securities and Exchange Commission, his income was not large. But it was large enough to enable him to carry on his social experiments.

"Perhaps, if I had done things differently," he said, "I might have accumulated millions, as did some of my contemporaries. In that case I would have had only a few years at most of the happiness that I've had most of my adult life.

"My friends have often told me that I do so many things that are unnecessary. I admit it. I have never wanted to be wealthy in terms of money. Maybe it's an impractical, idealistic strain inherited from my father, but it always seemed to me that the greatest wealth a man can attain is the happiness derived from the good will of his fellowmen. You can't buy that with money. You have to earn it—not in your spare time or after you've made your pile, as the saying goes, but by working for it all through life. It's a task that's never finished. That's what makes it so fascinating.

"I wish more people could see that and understand its value in terms of the only wealth worth striving for. I wish more people could see that it is the only indestructible wealth.

"It's not a case of being altruistic at all, for everything I've done has brought me gratification of individual expression and the great happiness of watching human development going on all around me. It's not a case of being either unselfish or impractical. It's actually selfish, and *most* practical; for I'm rich in so many ways that make life worth while that I've never desired great material wealth."

These remarks, uttered shortly after his seventy-fifth birthday, constitute his attempt to explain himself. Perhaps they explain less adequately than his actions—especially those in the later years of his life. For, after 1928 brought his release from burdensome personal debts, he was able to give more concentrated attention to creative thinking and planning. The younger men whom he had trained in his viewpoints had now moved up into positions of control in the company. Charles Hook, who had earned the highest place in the organization, had married his daughter Leah, and had now become his alter ego.

The board of strategy had long been dissatisfied with the geographic position of the Columbus blast furnaces. They were too far from the ore and coke sources and from the company's steel plants. In 1928 the condition was corrected with another pioneering achievement.

At New Miami, a small town between Hamilton and Middletown, there was a blast furnace on the site of what had been one of the first by-product coke ovens in the United States. Down through the years its owners had made many offers of co-operation. To all such offers, Verity always replied, "When we make any such change, we shall put our blast furnaces right alongside our steel plant in Middletown so that we can have full advantage of the use of molten metal." However, he considered it flagrant waste of natural resources to continue the old practice of putting the heat of coal into ore at blast furnaces and then letting such heat leak away in the manufacture and transportation to the steel-mill furnaces of cold pig iron. He had long wanted to know why molten iron from a blast furnace could not be tapped directly into the open-hearth furnace.

Finally, in collaboration with the Koppers Company and the Baltimore & Ohio Railroad, equipment was developed to make practical such an operation in the Hamilton location. The furnaces and coke ovens at New Miami were then bought and the Columbus operations were moved to this site.

On the morning of June 25, 1928, a group of distinguished guests, led by B. & O. President Daniel Willard, assembled in Verity's office to congratulate his company on another achievement. Boarding a special train at East Works, the party rode over a new railroad line linking the open-hearth department with the blast furnaces twelve miles away. At the blast furnace, the party watched the pouring of the first "cast" of molten iron into one of Armco's new "thermos-bottle" railroad cars. These insulated cars, resembling submarines, had been designed and built to transport molten iron without loss of heat. Because they concentrated loads of 300 tons on sixteen wheels within a space of only fifty-six feet, a new kind of railroad line had to be built to carry the heaviest wheel load ever moved over rails.

Returning to East Works, the party watched the submarine-on-wheels roll slowly on its side and disgorge its liquid fire into a ladle which then poured it directly into the open-hearth furnace.

That night there was a banquet in Middletown's Hotel Manchester to celebrate the event, but the guest of honor, present in body, was not present in spirit.

Among his intimate friends it was known that he was spending almost every night at the bedside of his old friend, "Duce" Phillips, who was seriously ill.

A few nights later, at an employees' garden party, he spoke briefly to the Armco workers.

"There is one thought I wish to leave with you," he said.

Hart, N. Y.

Charles Ruffin Hook, President of the American Rolling Mill Company.

To obtain special finishes, particularly desirable in the manufacture of automobiles, coils of cold steel more than 3,000 feet long are raced through the cold-strip mill.

"While we are here tonight in the fullness of life, let us remember that life moves swiftly and mysteriously, that many lives are coming in and many others going out in every hour of the day, and that if we are to have the sort of achievement that makes for happiness we must accomplish it *today.* We must get our happiness out of our work, our play and our association with friends and fellow workers today—not tomorrow.

"True, we must plan for tomorrow, but today is the day we *live.*

"We are here tonight in acknowledgement of the truth that *today,* not tomorrow, is our time of action."

Next day—July 11, 1928—death took old friend Phillips.

By 1929 the new processes introduced by the continuous mills had created so much labor displacement in steel mills throughout the country that labor union officials became alarmed. Because many of the old unionized crafts were either abolished or altered by the new techniques, new terms between Armco and its craftsmen were drawn up and signed in the presence of the national officers of the union. Sixty days later, these national officers asked the members of the Middletown lodge to abrogate their agreement. They refused. The officials then called upon them to strike. The men met, considered the strike order and voted to ignore it. Thus an old and valued association came to an end.

As the company had grown, the system of departmental advisory committees had been refined and improved. Members of such committees were elected by secret ballot for a year of service as the employees' representatives. These departmental committees elected members of works advisory committees who met once a month with the works management to present complaints and suggestions and receive reports on management's problems such as costs, orders, financial status of the company and management's opinions on the general state of business.

Though the system was intended to be not a formal representation plan or "company union," but rather a medium for maintaining close contact between management and men, it eventually became an effective means of employee representation.

In 1938, the National Labor Relations Board was asked by the Steel Workers' Organizing Committee of the C.I.O. for an election to determine whether employees in the Butler works desired a union to represent them. When the proposal of union representation was turned down by a majority of more than four to one, the S. W. O. C. organizers issued a statement commending the company for its fair attitude during the balloting.

Early in 1930, George Verity decided the time had come to give younger hands greater responsibilities in management and a chance at the controls of the company. Acting on his suggestions, the directorate named him its chairman, moved Charles Hook into the president's chair and raised Calvin Verity to the executive vice-presidency. With his detailed responsibilities thus lightened, he planned to examine some of the company's foreign outposts and devote himself mainly to problems of organization and company policy.

But this plan was not to be put into practice so quickly. Just as the depression set in, the company acquired, as a subsidiary company, the Sheffield Steel Corporation, with offices and plants in Kansas City, Missouri, and additional plants in Saint Louis and Oklahoma City.* The expanding of operations into manufacture of rod and wire products, increased the company's problems as the depression deepened. In the next three years all the efforts of Verity and his associates were required to fight back the specter of industrial collapse.

But even in these dark days the pioneering continued.

As early as 1930 it was becoming apparent to some of the strategists that a neglected frontier for American inventive ingenuity lay in the field of housing. In the housing of the American people they discerned a serious technological lag. While millions of words were spoken and written about the inadequacy of shelter, the extent and need of new construction and the obstacles barring Americans from acquiring dwellings even remotely comparable to, say, automobiles in cost per pound and value per dollar, the Verity associates quietly experimented with prefabricated shelter.

One of their experimental houses was a popular show place at the Century of Progress Exposition in Chicago. An enthusiastic public reaction to the famed Armco-Ferro-Enamel House indicated that it was at least a partial answer to the mounting demand for modern, efficient shelter. But it was a partial answer only, and the research was continued in Middletown.

As a result, the community's suburbs grew to resemble a

* Ground was broken in May, 1941, for another Sheffield unit in Houston, Texas.

town of the future. A growing collection of prefabricated steel houses, the fruits of the research, spread out over the landscaped hills. Most of these homes were planned and built for Armco employees who wanted to own their dwellings and knew that the shelter buyer gets much more for his dollar when he builds the modern type of structure.

By 1933 the prospects were brightening for the company. In 1934 the sun of promise shone again. And in 1935 sales and production rose above the previous records established in 1929.

Then Mr. and Mrs. Verity embarked on their long-deferred visit to Europe. After a delightful journey across the Continent they visited Pateley Bridge, the Verity homestead in the Vale of the Nid, in Yorkshire.

Returning in June, 1935, he turned his attention to some timbered land and eroded farms which he had bought originally for use as bridle paths by a group of Middletown's young people who had formed a riding club. During his sojourn in the peaceful English countryside where his ancestors had tended their acres, Verity had begun to revolve a new idea in connection with these farmlands of his. By the time he reached home the idea had become a plan.

Combining the timbered areas and the worn-out farms into a single tract, he launched a program of soil reclamation and rehabilitation which developed into Niderdale Farms, a five-hundred-acre combination of woodland park and dairy farm. Of this he said:

"I always like to plan and build. The most pleasant memories of my childhood are those moments when I planned and made things with a makeshift set of tools. Later I derived great pleasure from working out plans for the buildings and equipment required in our original plant and spreading them out on a surveyor's plat. As our plants became vast sprawling mazes, requiring the mature knowledge of experienced architects and engineers, the pleasure of that sort of planning was taken away from me. So I had to find other outlets. This was such an outlet.

"After I bought these extensive acres, I was land poor, but I was rewarded with much pleasure in the development of the farm. My grandsons, their friends and I got a lot of wholesome exercise in cutting paths and trails through the wooded canyons. My superintendent, Fred Ruscher, who was employed at my home and in farm construction work, is a man of wide experience in mechanical and practical things, who enjoyed the building of fences, water lines and roads. He particularly liked the stone construction work that went along with the working out of drainage problems. We spent many happy hours planning and building. And Mrs. Verity and I enjoyed many delightful summer days converting a swamp into a pool for wildfowl and building a camp for Girl Scouts."

All these things became adjuncts of the farm which, eventually stocked with a herd of a hundred Jerseys, became one of the best dairy farms in Ohio. Operated for him by a young couple whom he "dug up and turned loose on the place because they had some novel ideas about dairying which deserved encouragement," it repeatedly received highest awards at Ohio State Fairs.

There, in the late nineteen-thirties, he planned and built to his heart's content.

In these years, too, he found another outlet, not only for his love of the land and his urge to create, but for his pleasure in bringing satisfaction to as many people as possible. Around 1920 he had been offered a wooded, weed-choked group of ravines and gully-rutted hills at a price ridiculously low. Inspecting this five-hundred-acre tract in the highlands east of town, he had envisioned its possibilities as a park and urged the company's board of directors to purchase it.

After the company bought it, the site had lain undeveloped for a number of years. A few years before he was relieved of his presidential duties, he began to devote more time to his plan for reclaiming and developing this land. Under his direction the tract was transformed into Armco Park, a public playground of natural beauty, one of the finest natural parks in Ohio.

The park's central valley, once a public dump, was transformed into a popular recreation center by the addition of driven wells, picnic sites in shaded glens, tennis courts, playfields. Forest paths were laid out, and the trees labeled for nature study. The meadows and wooded dells were tied together by a motor road which climbs to a plateau providing an excellent view of the Miami Valley.

There is a dell in the park called "Bunny Hollow," a children's world never profaned by the heavy feet of adults. There is a fenced twenty-acre sanctuary for birds and small game. Near by is a camp for Girl Scouts, and a summer camp in which the Civic Association annually builds up the bodies of undernourished children.

About a hundred thousand persons use the park's many

facilities every summer; and, to Mr. Verity's great satisfaction, no misuse of it has ever necessitated the service of park policemen.

Unlike many such projects, this one was not shifted to the taxpayers. The park belongs to the company. The company maintains it, pays the salaries and wages of working personnel and throws the park open without restriction to anyone who wants to use it and not abuse it.

Adjacent to the park and belonging to it is a 160-acre tract, leased to the Wildwood Community Golf Club which operates an eighteen-hole course.

In the following years, similar parks were built in other Armco communities. In addition, the employees, operating through their Armco Association, developed athletic parks in all these communities for their field days and sports programs.

All these are the lengthening shadows of one man, the expressions of his pleasure in extending to all mankind the warmth of friendship.

Describing how Armco Park grew a bit at a time, he revealed an uncommon understanding of human perversity.

"In doing uncalled-for things for your fellow men," he said, "you must be careful not to do so much at one time that they feel indebted to you. People suspect you when you are too generous. The only way to do a thing of this kind is to launch it quietly and without display. If you do it in an attempt to sell yourself to the public, the public will find you out and you'll fail.

"You must proceed carefully, doing a little at a time, continue doing a little more, year in and year out, and never give in to the temptation to sit back and say it is finished.

"The mistake many businessmen make is that they think of the improvement of human relations as a part-time job. Actually it's the basic reason for their being in business. It *is* their business! It should be their full-time job.

"It's not enough to have working conditions satisfactory in the plant. If you're an employer, you must first of all be fair and honest with your employees. If you aren't, they will soon know it, and nothing you do is any good. The first requisite is a fair wage, the best possible under existing conditions. Then you must do everything else in your power to make your employees feel they are working with you and not for you, which they *must* feel to make your business a success. After you've done these things, you must extend your interest and activities into the community where your employees and their families live. Here, especially, you must guard against the antagonism of people who, when you do too much too suddenly, resent your efforts as intrusions into their private affairs.

"If you set up such a working schedule for yourself, how can you ever be so blind as to consider the job finished?

"No, the best part of all this is that it is never done. There's always the new adventure of more to be done tomorrow."

Verity's philosophic acceptance of even the untoward event as a new adventure manifested itself on December 28, 1935. Near twelve o'clock on that bitterly cold night, Middletown was shaken awake by a rumble and roar. In an eye-blink of time the

George M. Verity and John Hogan, Armco veteran, 1934.

George M. Verity, Charles F. Kettering and Charles R. Hook at the dedication of the new Armco Research Laboratory, 1937.

George M. Verity on his 75th birthday, April 22, 1940.

Armco Research Building became a rubbish pile, as gas, affected by a sudden change in temperature, flung the walls out and the roof up. The force of the blast smashed windows over a wide area of the town.

As company officials, summoned to the scene, stood around wringing their hands, Verity arrived.

"Was anyone hurt?" he asked.

Informed that nobody had been in or near the building at the time of the explosion, his face brightened.

"Good!" he exclaimed. "Could we have prevented it?"

"Apparently not," was the reply.

"Let's not worry about it then," he said. "We'll build another one—a better one!"

Then he ordered the entire available personnel to conduct a house-to-house survey of damage in the community, and carpenters and glaziers were promptly repairing the town's broken windows on company orders.

A few days later he assembled a committee to make a thorough study of the company's research needs and an exhaustive survey of the whole field of industrial research. This committee included Dr. Anson Hayes, chemist and former member of Iowa State College, who later became Armco's research director.

The ultimate result was a new research building, a magnificent structure of stainless steel, porcelain-enameled panels and glass brick, with twelve completely equipped laboratories. Dedicated on November 5, 1937, with ceremonies attended by more than two hundred scientists, engineers, industrialists and editors from all over the country, it was inspected by more than nine thousand visitors in the first three days after it was opened.

At the dedication ceremonies, Charles F. ("Boss Kett") Kettering, General Motors Corporation's vice president said:

"My hat is off to Mr. Verity and his associates because in times like these, when certain people are looking very gloomily into the future, it is a breath of romance to smell a new research laboratory."

In this building, the very walls of which are wrought of many materials which earlier Armco research made possible, the Verity strategists today chart tomorrow's battles against the enemies and weaknesses of metal alloys. Here, in recent years, means have been developed to combine the toughness of steel with the corrosion-resistance of zinc and aluminum, paints and bitumen, and the superior qualities of organic plastics.

Here, too, was done part of the research that developed the tremendously significant "anodic" polishing method by which lustrous metal surfaces are produced semi-automatically and inexpensively. The process, sometimes called "electroplating-in-reverse," was developed in collaboration with the Rustless Iron & Steel Corporation of Baltimore, the company which controls patents on the simplest and shortest method of making stainless steel and in which Armco acquired a substantial interest in 1937.

Out of Armco's laboratories also, in 1939, came methods and mechanism for welding silicon steel, an achievement which resulted in large savings to transformer manufacturers and electric power consumers.

23

Steel Without Strife

In 1935 George Verity reached that seventieth milestone beyond which tradition holds that men should rest. In theory, he was retired from active duty. In fact, he continued in harness more active than ever, adhering to his old habit of arising at dawn for an early-morning canter, and arriving at his desk at least a half hour before the office employees, in order "to get a lot of work done before the interruptions begin."

On Thanksgiving Day of that year a tall silver vase was placed on his desk, flower-filled. There was no explanation save that it was from the general office employees, "in token of appreciation to one who never hesitates to take time to do things for others." Next day it was filled with fresh flowers—and next day and next day and every working day thereafter. Those who presented it pledged to continue filling it daily "from now on."

"It's magnificent," he said. "Magnificent—but embarrassing. No one can merit this tribute."

Thereafter his office began to take on the appearance of a museum as the months and years brought additional tokens of appreciation from his many friends.

"In recent years," he said, "every day has been as Christmas to me. The motives, the affection behind these expressions are the real rewards of life."

It has been remarked often that one of the prices industry must pay for bigness is the loss of that intimate contact between management and men which is natural in the small shop but not in the large organization. Verity found and fostered many measures to prevent gulfs between executives and employees. Among these was the formation of veterans' clubs for the exceptionally large proportion of employees with long service records. Of the company's 13,000 employees in 1939, the average age was 38.73 years, the average length of service was 9.2 years, and 623 had service records of more than twenty-five years.

Many awards have been established with which outstanding achievements are accorded official recognition—a host of safety awards topped by "the Iron Man," the bronze statue of a steelworker, made by the late Clement L. Barnhorn, Cincinnati sculptor, which is awarded annually to the operating unit with the best safety record. Also, there is the Armco Distinguished Service award, now given for heroism, which grew out of an earlier custom of giving medal awards for outstanding sportsmanship.

Other influences that tend to bind the organization together are the advisory committees and the Armco Association. The latter group, which began as a mutual-benefit insurance society, expanded its social and recreational activities after 1913. As communities containing company branches developed better facilities for recreation, the social importance of the Association diminished and the emphasis shifted to athletics. In every community containing an operating unit, the Association maintains an athletic field and sponsors field days and regular schedules of baseball and basketball. During its long history, this readily adaptable organization has staged music and drama festivals, organized bands and orchestras, developed musicians and sponsored clubs for foreign and Negro workers. In Nellis, West Virginia, where the company acquired coal mines and had to build and operate an entire community for the miners' families, the Association supplies virtually all the town's social and recreational needs, even maintaining a golf course in the mountains.

The company guards its human assets carefully and diligently, as it watches its balance sheet. One of the most important units in the organization is the personal service department, which supervises the manifold "social" services. In years when foreign labor was plentiful, it provided citizenship training. It instituted an employees' school in which as many as eighteen hundred students in one season took courses ranging from addition to calculus, coal-stoking to mining engineering, blueprint reading to metallography.

In 1940, when the needs of American defense resulted in a government order to build a huge aircraft engine factory at Lockland, Ohio, and the question arose as to the supply of skilled craftsmen to man the factory's machines, Armco's president, Charles Hook, offered his company's training facilities and ordered the general-office garage in Middletown converted into classrooms and workshop for the trainees.

When the influx of foreign labor was shut off in 1914 and Negroes came north to fill the gap, the personal service department housed the men until shelter could be provided for their families, and set up schools to overcome their illiteracy and help them become good citizens. At a cost of $60,000, the company built Booker T. Washington School for their children and presented it to the Middletown Board of Education. In addition, it hired Negro social workers, provided playgrounds for the children and sponsored formation of Negro clubs.

Similar social work was done to weld into the community the large numbers of Kentucky and Tennessee hillfolk attracted to the plant during and after the war.

If a community in which the company operates has a need which the community cannot serve, the department investigates and tries to fill the bill, whether the need is a playground, a park, better recreational facilities, housing or gardens. To overcome a housing shortage in Ashland, the company built fifty homes for sale at cost to employees. Each of the Armco plants is beautified as much as possible with lawns, flowers, trees and shrubbery, and garden tracts for employees have been supplied regularly since 1913, when Verity inaugurated the practice which became common in many industries and communities in the 1930's.

Sometimes the personal service department gets a request it cannot handle. One such was a persistent employee demand in 1917 that the company operate a bank on the premises. After thorough consideration, the directors deemed it unwise, but satisfied the employees by constructing a bank building on plant property at East Works which was turned over to one of Middletown's banks for operation as a branch. Later, also with the assistance of this department, the employees organized their own credit unions, one of which became the largest in Ohio.

Personal Service does not try to interfere in the lives of the men. It merely applies the Verity doctrine: "People are helped best who help one another most." Its success is due in large measure to the fact that George Verity succeeded in transferring his ideas and ideals to the key men in the management. Various and sometimes seemingly irrelevant were the means he employed in order to see men demonstrate their ability to understand his theories before advancement to positions of responsibility.

In his search for promising young men in the company, he had lists of names prepared for his use. Regularly, he picked men from these lists, invited them to his home with their wives and became acquainted with them by taking them to dinner and the theater. Another method he employed to counteract the disintegrating forces of corporate growth was a series of summer garden parties at his home. To these he devoted one evening each fortnight, inviting all employees of one department and their families each time.

It was natural that the Verity influence should reach out and transform communities eventually. The effects are apparent especially in Middletown.

The town is aptly named. Bearing little trace of either abject poverty or showy wealth, it is eminently middle-class. Because its principal industry is Armco, it is a mill town. But it is not a *typical* mill town. It has none of the frigid, regimented uniformity of those paternalistic mill towns called "model" towns. Nor has it the clammy, ramshackle disorder of those monstrous muddle-towns—the architectural trash heaps that surround too many American steel mills. It is a middle-town, as middle-class as apple pie for supper, as middle-American as Old Man River.

Though its population is an amalgam of many nationalities, races and creeds, its people are neighborly and notably free of factional strife. Though one of every seven of its inhabitants is an Armco employee, it bears no aspect of a town tied to a mill.

Fortunately situated, in beautifully rolling country, with fertile farmlands near by, the town has spread far beyond its corporate limits. Within these limits, one finds none of the squalor, dirt, slovenliness and slum conditions common to industrial towns. Even in the older sections, the "General Grant Gothic" façades are freshly painted and the surrounding grounds are well-groomed lawns and gardens.

Outside the limits, for mile after rolling mile, people who call themselves Middletonians live in homes among the hills. Some are simply homes in the country. Some are profitable farms, not a few of which are owned by Armco men who have retired.

The essence of the town's uniqueness inheres in the fact that, in a nation in which fewer than forty-four of every one hundred homes are owned by the people who dwell in them, sixty-four of every one hundred Middletown homes are owned by their occupants.

This is the town which was a disintegrating community forty years ago and which began to become a community in earnest only twenty-five years ago.

Spontaneously, in 1936, the people of this community declared a holiday to honor the man they credited with the large share of the transformation.

On Saturday, June 6th, Middletonians—all thirty-thousand

of them—invited neighboring communities to help them celebrate "Verity Day." Ten thousand of them marched.

Faced with this display of community esteem, words almost failed the honored citizen for the first time in his life.

Former Governor James Middleton Cox, who passed his youth in the community, participated in the program. This onetime presidential nominee observed: "George Verity's outstanding quality is his ability to make people forget their prejudices. I saw today a symbol of the spirit he has engendered. In the line of march I saw old Father Gerdes [Monsignor A. M. Gerdes], bearing the weight of four-score years, meeting the exactions of the long tramp to the reviewing stands, a representative of the Pope doing honor to the son of an old-time, saddle-bag minister."

Of the demonstration, the man himself said:

"No man has ever had more appreciation for what little he has done than I have. I can accept these honors only because I know that in the minds of people who bestow them I am merely a symbol of things *we* have done together in co-operative effort. What we have created here is too tremendous to have been done by any one man."

On his seventy-fifth birthday George Verity ignored all the warnings of his family, escaped into the country, saddled and mounted his favorite horse and rode the animal over the hurdles. To mark the event, he had a companion photograph it. When members of his family saw the picture, they forced him to promise not to repeat the performance.

"I promise," he said, "—until my eightieth birthday!"

On July 4, 1940, editor B. C. Forbes had come to Middletown to officiate at the formal presentation of the "Humanizer of Business" award for which George Verity had been selected by a committee of businessmen, scientists, sociologists and editors. In the Verity living room Forbes was spinning a humorous yarn in that faintly Aberdonian burr of his, when the front door opened to admit a delegation of steelworkers. Addressing Forbes, their spokesman announced: "In return for the honor you have bestowed on our friend, we have decided to name you the first honorary Armco man."

After they presented him with a miniature reproduction of "the Iron Man," Forbes indulged in a bit of reminiscence.

"I don't think I need to remind anyone here that the steel industry has had a particularly unsavory reputation for having been headed by tough babies," he said. "I've known most of the heads of this industry personally. Seeing you workmen in this home, I've been thinking how utterly unlikely such a gathering would have been in the homes of some of the autocrats I've known.

"Ever since I started *Forbes' Magazine* I've striven to show industrialists the value of the line of conduct typical here. At the masthead of every issue I've put the Biblical admonition: 'With all thy getting get understanding.' If only fifty-one per cent of the nation's industrialists could learn the value of the Verity formula, and apply it, we should not have to fear for the future of America."

In the conversation that followed, George Verity said the Forbes masthead quotation summed up perfectly the basic truth he had been trying to get into men's minds since his start in the business.

"There has always been a general recognition of the value of co-operation in America," he said. "We all realize that our nation could not have been built without it. All businessmen have talked about it for years. But it seems hard for even the people who talk about it to see that it isn't worth-while unless it comes through good will and mutual understanding.

"The dictators in the totalitarian nations have a short-cut to co-operation. It is very effective—frightfully effective! Its effectiveness presents free men with a dreadful challenge.

"Now we *must* attain co-operation. Unless we do so much better than we have done in the past, our freedom will be seriously endangered; for the benefits of co-operation are now being demonstrated with such frightful force in Europe that none of us can afford to miss the meaning. I fear that unless we Americans learn to co-operate through the good will that comes from understanding, we shall have it forced upon us, paying for it with our freedom.

"That would be a high price to pay for it—too high a price, I believe. For the worth of anything can be measured by what it brings. If co-operation must be bought with freedom, it isn't worth the cost. On the other hand, if understanding can bring it without endangering freedom, then it should be plain that persistent effort to understand our fellow men has a definite and known value to all of us."

Francis Bacon held that Nature must be obeyed to be commanded. Though he referred to external nature, his doctrine is true of human nature. The one big mistake of the nineteenth century was the attempt to change human nature without understanding the laws of change. The problems now confronting civilized man stem directly from our elders' attempts to impose new habits and customs on human beings without trying to understand how men must be adapted to new social patterns in order to give stability to such patterns.

George Verity strove to achieve such understanding.

His chief pride lay in the fact that, in more than forty years, misunderstanding between management and men had not cost his company one ounce of lost production nor his men one cent of lost wages. Disclaiming recognition as a steelmaker with the remark, "My chief interest has always been human beings," he nevertheless achieved the distinction of having made steel without strife.

It is a rare distinction.

That it has been done is occasion for hope that the magnificent material gains obtained by mankind at enormous cost of human effort in the age of steel may yet be saved by inherently freedom-loving, oppression-hating Americans to implement a better world for posterity.

That it has been done in—of all places!—the steel industry, which has furnished all too many dark and sordid chapters in industrial history, seems to indicate that there may be many additional possibilities, still unexplored, in deliberate attempts to produce true steel by alloying honesty with iron.

As these words are written, crisis again confronts America.

As in that despairful April when George Matthew Verity was born, men are saying:

"It is the end."

The end of what? Civilization? What is civilization but the task of humanizing humanity? And that task, as George Verity observed, is endless.

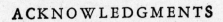

ACKNOWLEDGMENTS

Acknowledgments

BEFORE I bow out, there are a few acknowledgments to be made. So, here I want to express my thanks to:

Pendleton Dudley, who nudged my curiosity in the first place;

Rosemary York, Jessica Mannon and Andrew H. Hepburn, whose enthusiasms were so infectious that I succumbed to curiosity;

Hugh W. Wright and all his Armco associates, who tolerated my sometimes impolite skepticism, answered my blunt questions with light when they must have been tempted often to apply heat, and opened records to me when I demanded information or expressed doubts.

To all these my thanks—and apologies for the limitation of space that militates against the listing of scores of names.

Thanks, especially, to those "nobodies that do the work" in the mills, factories and offices where I discovered ample proof that the "Armco spirit" of which these workers speak is a very real and lively force. I cannot hope to repay these people for their remarkable patience with an inordinately inquisitive busybody who must have tested their patience mightily with his unabashed ignorance and granite-headed misconceptions. I can only hope that what I have written about the man whom they call friend is at least a partial repayment for their many kindnesses.

Heartfelt thanks, too, to the old settlers, the newspapermen and the librarians in those Ohio communities where I followed the fading trail of the Verity boyhood wanderings; and to the many Middletonians who contributed valuable information—sometimes, I suspect, without knowing that my queries were not merely expressions of idle curiosity.

Thanks, too, to William McFee, Harry Mercer, W. W. Sebald, Charles Murray, Ed Schmid, Tim Sullivan, Dean Phillips and Mrs. Alta Smith for their candid criticism of the work in progress; and to David Laurance Chambers whose knack of pummeling fat and flabby pages into lean paragraphs invariably evokes my greenest envy.

I owe much also to many other writers, the pockets of whose minds I have picked in that unconscious form of theft of which all who write are guilty. For to read is to remember, and to write is to string together on a new cord the plunder hoarded in the attic of memory.

"Taking something from a man and making it worse," said George Moore, "is plagiarism."

The stench of that sin I hope I shall not have to scrub off my conscience. But, if I have unwittingly committed it, the fault is mine alone. Of those persons to whom I have acknowledged indebtedness, none is to be held responsible for the use I have made of the information furnished.

Christy Borth

Parshallville, R. 3,
Fenton, Michigan

INDEX

INDEX